Living Large
in Small Spaces

EXPRESSING PERSONAL STYLE IN
100 TO 1,000 SQUARE FEET

BY MARISA BARTOLUCCI

PHOTOGRAPHY BY RADEK KURZAJ

Harry N. Abrams, Inc., Publishers

100 sf
200 sf
300 sf
350 sf
400 sf
450 sf
500 sf
600 sf
750 sf
800 sf
900 sf
1000 sf

Contents

8 INTRODUCTION

THE LIVING SPACES

100 SQUARE FEET
30   The Dormitory Room of Yen Feng

200 SQUARE FEET
40   The Studio of Shane Ruth

300 SQUARE FEET
52   The Studio of Christopher Coleman
62   The Studio of Jorge Vargas

350 SQUARE FEET
72   The Studio of William Stewart and John Dyer

400 SQUARE FEET
82   The One-Bedroom Apartment of Judy Hudson and Stuart Basseches
94   The Studio of Stephen Earle
102   The Studio of Virginia Briggs

450 SQUARE FEET
110   The Studio of Leslie Hoffman
120   The Studio of Mary Trasko
130   The Studio of Donald Albrecht
140   The Studio of Francisco Pardo and Ximena Orozco

500 SQUARE FEET
150   The One-Bedroom Apartment of Isabelle Bosquet
160   The Studio of Jeffrey Shertz
170   The One-Bedroom Apartment of Jordan Schaps
176   The One-Bedroom Apartment of Livia Kamberos

600 SQUARE FEET

184 The One-Bedroom Apartment of Sonia Harris

194 The One-Bedroom Apartment of Will Van Roden and Anthony Lee

208 The One-Bedroom Apartment of Wing Chan

220 The One-Bedroom Apartment of Lotta Jansdotter

750 SQUARE FEET

232 The One-Bedroom Apartment of Ruby Lerner

800 SQUARE FEET

246 The One-Bedroom Bungalow of Steven Shortridge

258 The Converted Loft of Deborah Oropallo and Michael Goldin

268 The One-Bedroom Apartment of Laura Handler

280 The One-Bedroom Apartment of Thomas Dang Vu and Allan Kam

292 The Two-Bedroom Apartment of Raul Cabra, Luis Catala, and Michael Sledge

308 The One-Bedroom Shotgun House of Bert Long and Joan Batson

318 The One-Bedroom Apartment of Ken Kennedy and Judith Curr

900 SQUARE FEET

332 The Two-Bedroom Apartment of Mark Rabiner and Avi Pemper

1,000 SQUARE FEET

350 The Two-Bedroom Garden Apartment of Michael Webb

362 The Two-Bedroom Loft of Keira Alexandra

372 The One-Bedroom Garden Apartment of Antonio Da Motta and Robert Ketterman

382 The One-Bedroom Apartment of Karen Meyer

396 DIRECTORY OF FEATURED DESIGN PROFESSIONALS

398 CREDITS

Introduction

No matter what place in the world you call home, when it comes to urban living arrangements, space is a luxury. In Japan, this has been a fact of life for so long, living compactly has become an art form; in Europe, it's the norm. But in America, because of our inherited sense of the Great Frontier, we consider spacious dwellings—even in cities—a birthright, so most of us struggle with the notion of living small. Nevertheless, the National Apartment Association reported in 2001 that the average apartment in America was some 800 square feet. If you've ever searched for an apartment in any of the more densely populated American cities, such as San Francisco, Los Angeles, Houston, or Chicago, chances are you will recognize an apartment of this size as being livable but not particularly roomy, especially when

Today, more and more of us live in cities where space is an increasingly precious commodity, as this aerial view of Tokyo shows. Even in more rural towns like California's Mendocino, open space is fast disappearing.

accommodating more than one person. In New York City, the square footage of a typical one-bedroom is a little more than half that size! Despite such data, the worlds of advertising, television, and films besiege us with images of average people living in ample, well-appointed houses. All this make-believe only sharpens reality's pinch. But there's no need to sing the real-estate blues. With a change of attitude, it is possible to live large in small spaces.

Accepting smallness is the first step to living large. A little home needn't be a cause for embarrassment. Consider it a lifestyle choice, not a financial necessity. It's a liberating shift in mind-set—and lifestyle—because in truth small spaces are more freeing. A number of the small-home dwellers featured in this book could afford more square footage. They choose to live in condensed spaces because such spaces are easier to care for and are more efficient. As urbanites, they see the city as an extension of their dwellings. Restaurants, hotels, cinemas, theaters, clubs, gyms, and even some retail environments contain areas that serve as living rooms. What they require in

As city homes shrink in size, restaurants, clubs, and hotel lobbies have begun to take the place of living rooms for urbanites. In Philadelphia, the restaurant Pod, below left, resembles a lounge. In New York City, the lobby of W Union Square hotel, opposite, looks like a luxurious private library, while the lobby of Chambers hotel, below, was designed to resemble the living room of a private art collector.

an actual home is a welcome place to relax and to sleep. With some ingenuity and esprit, a few also manage to entertain quite grandly.

Many small-home dwellers also appreciate the more personal nature of
their abodes. Unlike big spaces, little ones can be neatly fashioned to meet
individual needs, routines, and whims, so that they fit one's life as trimly as
a bespoke suit. As one's sense of style or living pattern changes, it takes
little effort and expense to alter the design and organization of such spaces.
They can evolve along with you much more gracefully than a large home
could.

To live large in a small space, then, you have to have the courage of your
design convictions, not those of an interiors book or a shelter magazine.
This book hopes to show that, like all interesting people and places, the best
little abodes are idiosyncratic. That's why this book offers up living spaces
that range in style from minimalist to grandma-cozy. It has been conceived
not so much as a guide, but as a source of inspiration for making the most
of what you have.

A Word on Smallness and Invention

In Gaston Bachelard's book *The Poetics of Space*, he reflects on the roman-
tic resonance of the hermit's hut. Ever since humankind began building
great houses, it seems we have waxed nostalgic about tiny, humble ones.
Why the longing? The truth of the hermit's hut, Bachelard muses, "must
derive from the intensity of its essence, which is the essence of the verb 'to
inhabit.'" This distillation of psychology and behavior is why making little
shelters has always been a favorite pastime for children and a choice project
for artists and architects. It is a way to explore and define the self. The spatial restrictions become a resource for personal invention.

Allan Wexler, an artist and architect, explores the patterns of daily existence
by building reductive shelters. One of his works, the *Vinyl Milford House*, is a
mass-produced utility shed that has been transformed into a modern-day
hermit's hut. All the equipment needed for daily life, a bed, a table and
chairs, and bathing and kitchen equipment, are stored away in like-shaped
crates inserted into the walls. When the occupant wants to sleep, the bed is
pulled out from the wall into the empty room; when dining is desired, the

Wexler's Vinyl Milford House
plays with the notions of
utility and size In a home.

bed is slid away to make space for the table and chairs. Wexler's shed is a study in ritualized efficiency. Yet the routines it examines are not very different from those of an apartment dweller living in a studio with a sofabed.

The idea of "living in a capsule" is a recurrent theme in artist Andrea Zittel's work, too. In *Travel Trailers*, three couples drove between San Diego and San Francisco towing specially designed campers. The trailers were just twelve-feet long and seven-and-a-half-feet wide and tall. Zittel wanted to see if their teeny, highly functional, and thoroughly standardized interiors, measuring just eighty-four square feet, could be made more domestic. She added custom features according to the tastes and requirements of each

couple. She changed the dining banquette into a lounge bed with a kid-
ney-shaped tray table in one; she added some potted plants and a
bathroom door with a porthole in the second; and she provided the
third, for a couple with a baby, with a diaper-changing table and
kitchen cabinets carved with a cartoon face. According to the different
couples, each of whom spent a few weeks living in the trailers, these
few potent details helped transform the impersonal layouts into invit-
ingly diminutive homes.

Zittel experimented with further compressing the living space in another, admittedly less appealing, work called the *Body Processing Unit*,
which was a booth-sized dwelling with a toilet, a shower, and a shelf for
eating. When these activities commingle this closely in a space, most
people experience it as repellent, not cozy. Zittel is playing with cultural
norms and our sensibilities (not to mention true issues of hygiene),
which are shaped much more by the era in which we live than we probably like to think. Before there was indoor plumbing, most people kept
a chamber pot under their bed. At the turn of the last century, most
tenement flats had tubs in the kitchen. Today, it's become quite trendy
to have a freestanding bathtub in the master bedroom. One of the
small-space dwellers profiled in this book built his bed into his ornately
outfitted bathroom. It's an unusual configuration to be sure, but it suits
him fine. Ignore convention and organize your space according to what
works for you, and you will be well on your way to living large.

For her parents, Zittel designed a Travel Trailer that resembles their boat's cabin. Simple accessories like a Mola hanging and hammock-strung string bag recall their love of tropical ports.

Zittel's personal Travel
Trailer includes a banquette
for lounging and a circular
bed tray.

Zittel confesses that she is fascinated with minihabitats because they offer a way "to live a liberated life." [1] This is why, since time immemorial, the young and bohemian have made their homes in cramped garrets, or in the case of Yolande Daniels and Sunil Bald, in a tiny, derelict Manhattan storefront. These two young architects wanted to experiment with a personalized living system. Their "lab" was a 300-square-foot, very narrow and totally open space, dark and dank with stone and brick walls and a concrete floor. Part of their experiment entailed using the "sidewalk economy" whenever

[1] Andrea Zittel, Gabrius Sp, Milan, 2002

The Flip Flop House

To dispel the gloom of the below-ground space, Daniels and Bald ran strips of fluorescents along the dirt grooves between the concrete floors and the walls. A big, round copper pot found at a nearby kitchen supply store was transformed into a fanciful bathtub. With a custom-made wooden frame, they constructed a Murphy bed with pneumatic hinges. Cantilevering a triangular piece of glass out of a niche in the wall and supporting it with a leg made from a steel pipe created a dining table. To screen the toilet, a discarded box-spring frame was placed between it and the tub, and electric bulbs were inserted in the box springs' coils to create a luminous wall. Determined not to let the frivolities of life distract them from their architectural work, Daniels

Opposite, a view of the Murphy bed when down.

Below, the gray block is the Murphy bed when stowed away. On the opposite wall is the couple's Week-at-a-Glance (WAAG) storage unit.

and Bald also experimented with wearing uniforms, color-coordinated to the days of the week. They stored them in a "WAAG" (Week-at-a-Glance storage unit), composed of a series of seven large, color-coded Rubber Maid containers bolted to the wall. The couple named their creation the Flip Flop House, and when they moved, they packed it up and took it along. They've modified it since to fit their different living spaces and their changing lives. The Flip Flop House may be hard-edged and minimalist, but it remains their very personal, highly resourceful solution to the requirements of daily life.

they could in converting the old storefront into a home. Whatever else they needed came off the shelves of hardware stores. Since it was a temporary accommodation, they didn't invest much in the space itself, but in its furnishings.

Through these furnishings Daniels and Bald defined the different activities within the space. Using furniture for architectural ends is sometimes the only economical way for renters to deal with a shoebox-size space. It's a strategy even the architectural giant Le Corbusier used in Le Petit Cabanon. This vacation retreat in the South of France was the only dwelling he ever built for himself and his wife. Although he was already a world-renowned architect when he set about building his beach house, he still designed a structure that was just twelve feet by twelve feet, no bigger than a hermit's hut. Clad in split logs, it looks like one, too. While it may have been roughly fashioned, Le Corbusier's design for the cabin deftly addressed each gesture of daily life through the scale and arrangement of its crude furnishings and equipment. With this little hut, he captured the intense essence of habitation, and as Bachelard suggests, there may be no more satisfying architectural experience. Happily, this is an experience any small-space dweller can aspire to with thrift-shop finds and some creative arranging.

The only house Le Corbusier ever built for himself was a humble cottage in the south of France. He called it "Le Petit Cabanon."

Le Corbusier used furniture
and fixtures to define the
space within his little cabin.

Assessing a Space, Assessing Yourself

What you value in a living space becomes apparent as soon as you start perusing the real-estate listings. Do you perk up at "big kitchen" or "outdoor space"? Does the home abounding in natural light catch your fancy, or the one with copious closets? Consider your preferences before you choose a new home. Is what you value rooted in how you will really live in this dwelling, or is it some fantasy of how you would like to? When surroundings are cramped, it's essential that you focus on what is truly fundamental to your happiness. So when you consider closets more important than natural light, think twice about whether you really wear all those shoes. If you're after a "real" kitchen so that you can give dinner parties, make certain you're equally enthusiastic about actually cooking and cleaning. With a small kitchen you can still have dinner parties, just order take-out food. In this regard, selecting a small home is much like therapy—it requires drilling down to get at the real you.

When assessing the livability of a small space, you need also consider whether its design will still feel open and attractive once it's filled with your furniture. What will the circulation be like? Remember that how freely you move through furnished space affects your experience of it. Clear paths give a sense of ease and openness; obstacle courses induce claustrophobia. If much of the space will be tightly arranged, make sure there will be enough room for an uncluttered nook for relaxing. If you want good natural light in your home, make sure it will be there when you are, not when you are at work! If you will be working at home, check to see if there is a cheery, comfortable corner for your office, big enough not just for your desk but for office equipment and supplies. Make sure it will be far enough away from your sleeping area to minimize stress at night and temptations to nap during the day.

Le Corbusier's seemingly
curious placement of small
windows throughout his
cabin had a purpose: to
frame like a jeweler the glorious views outside.

There May Be Guidelines, There Are No Rules

Most architects and designers will tell you to look for an interior with a varied plan, even if the dimensions are tiny. Basic architectural elements such as a foyer, a dressing room, a separate kitchen with a door, an elevated level, do add visual interest and surprise. Still, boxy spaces in their very blankness afford all sorts of possibilities for design and decorative interventions. If the empty storefront occupied by Daniels and Bald hadn't been so raw, they would never have been so daring in their design. A dwelling's character often derives from the improvisations on its apparent limitations. In this book, one small-space dweller painted big, boldly colored stripes on one of the walls of his teeny apartment to give it some masculine oomph, while another made space for a desk and a walk-in closet in her cramped home by suspending the bed from the ceiling! The great thing about small spaces is that they lend themselves to design experimentation.

Of course there are countless maxims for making the most of a small space: paint it white; go minimal; choose low furnishings. As the case studies in this book reveal, the contrary to each of these maxims can also be true. While there may be no rules to living large in a small space, there is no question it requires discipline. You do have to limit your possessions. Assessing what you really need and what you don't becomes an ongoing practice. And for those with less than the steely fortitude required, there's always self-storage.

If any advice about living in a small space rings true every time, it may simply be to proceed slowly in the design and furnishing. The longer you inhabit the space, the more you will understand the way you live in it. Spaces, like people, should evolve. In discussing the architecture of the home, the brilliant designer Eileen Gray may have put it best: "Formulas are nothing. Life is everything."

the living

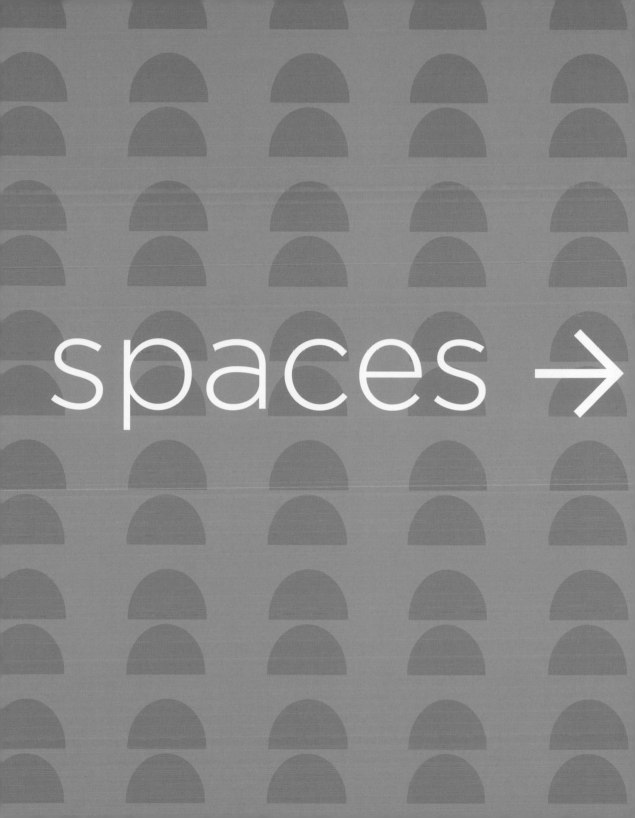

spaces →

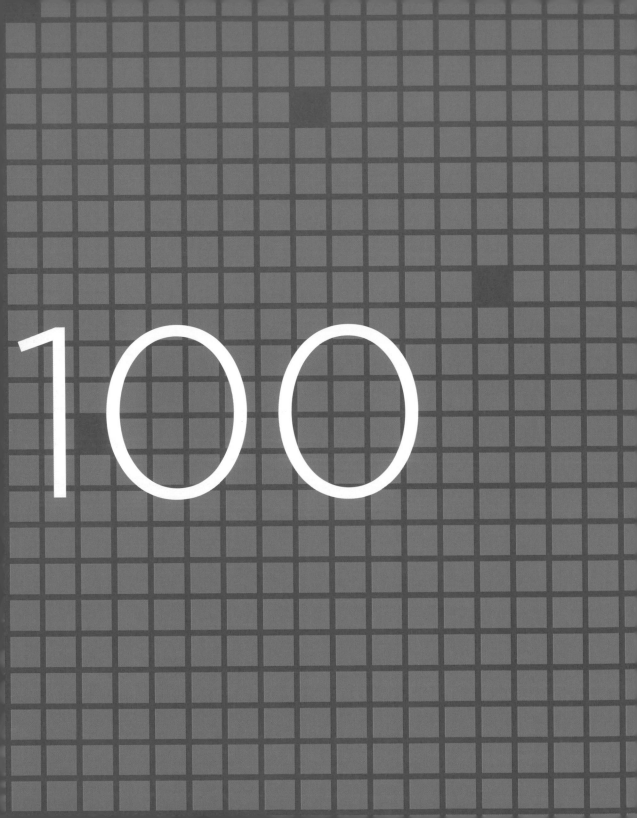

100

100 SF

YEN FENG

The first chance most of us get to freely decorate our own space is when we go off to college. When Yen Feng left his native Singapore to become a freshman at New York's Columbia University, he couldn't wait to have a room of his own. He'd grown up sharing a bedroom with two brothers in a small apartment and then for two years lived in an army barracks with thirteen other soldiers. Traveling halfway around the world, Feng couldn't bring with him much more than a few suitcases of clothes. In truth, there wasn't room for much else.

As he set about creating different zones within the tiny space for different activities, Feng quickly discovered that spatial organization could be a personalizing tool. "Order is important to me," he says. "By nature I'm very

Like necessity, a lack of space can be the Mother of Invention. Here, Feng turned an unneeded bed frame into a handy storage rack. This unconventional use of an everyday object gives the room some funk.

fussy about neatness and cleanliness." Even though he couldn't afford the kinds of trendy accessories with which he had first hoped to decorate his room, he recognized that by creating a tidily arranged space he was revealing much about himself. Growing more confident in organizing his room, Feng began to improvise, removing his mattress from the bed frame and placing it on the floor Japanese-style. By introducing a more complex sense of scale, he was able to better define his approximately one-hundred-square-feet into areas of work and rest. And with the bed on the floor, the room simply looked bigger. Feng was going to dispose of the bed frame, propping it up against the wall in the meantime, but as he went about arranging his possessions he discovered it made a convenient storage unit, especially for shoes. So he kept it there.

Multiple spatial levels create distinct zones within the minute room: the floor is for relaxing and sleeping; the desk is for working and eating; and the space by the ceiling is for showing off cards from family and friends.

What the room lacked, of course, were more sentimental details, objects from home. Feng made up for this by turning the very letters he got from family and friends into part of the room's decor. He pinned letters to the wall and strung cards across the room. When he got sick, his new school chums took care of him and brought him stuffed animals. Scattered about his bed, these toys add to the room's emotional resonance. The other decorative additions are modest but telling. Feng covered the surface of his wooden desk in aluminum foil to make it look more "techy," less "homespun." He plastered the wall with advertising images that appealed to him, maps of the world and of Manhattan, even business cards from the stores he frequented—banal adornments to us, perhaps, but exotic tokens for a Singapore lad in America for the first time.

When a space is tight and storage is minimal *and* exposed, everyday items often become the decor. These can be personally revealing. The objects in Feng's room speak of his new life in New York and recall distant loved ones.

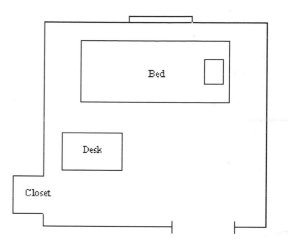

Feng covered his college-issue desk with aluminum foil to give it "a high-tech look."

A subway map of New York City, right, decorates a wall.

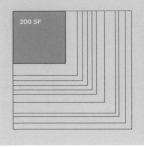

200 SF

SHANE RUTH

Shane Ruth's 200-square-foot apartment on New York City's Restaurant Row is about as space-challenged as a studio can be. When he first moved in, the aspiring artist had just taken a position in the display department of an exclusive Manhattan department store. He didn't have much money, so he built most of the furnishings himself. He placed inexpensive automobile air filters over the recessed spots to diffuse the light and provide some chic. He hammered together a big wooden desk. In order to separate the kitchen from the living area, he constructed a screen out of some lumber, bolts,

A chair by Mies van der Rohe, a cuckoo clock, mini-cowboy boots, and an industrial-style desk, all in one corner? Why not? If you have an eclectic vision, express it boldly without concern for the conventions of taste. True personal style always takes risks.

and a two-way mirror, which he scrounged from the store's prop department. (Inventive Ruth may be, but his degree in industrial design cannot be
discounted.) While his apartment was now more livable, it wasn't really a
fully functional home. Ruth's full-size bed still dominated. He seldom asked
friends over because, as he explains, "it would have been like inviting people
into my bedroom." In fact it was. But being a recluse didn't bother him.
When Ruth was home, he was busy painting, illustrating, or making vitrine
vignettes.

After a few years, though, he bought a Murphy bed. "It changed my life,"
Ruth says. "It gave me head space." (In other words, a living room.) By then
he'd also found his own style. It seems to have emerged out of his new ease
with his multiple identities as a design sophisticate, artist, and, by his own
description, "woodsy nature boy." These various identities wove themselves
together organically as he began decorating his new living area. Over time,
he bought some stylish props from the store: a classic Modernist loveseat; a
chic stainless-steel cabinet for his CDs; and a "tribal" tray table. He painted

Ruth hid his Murphy bed
behind a screen made of deer
netting, so it would blend in
with the sylvan decor.

The window blinds, made
from brown felt, are also his
creation.

Modern elements—the metal bar stool, sideboard, and couch—live cozily amidst Ruth's rustic collections of hunting trophies, anatomical drawings, and his own thorny paintings and vignettes.

His taste makes edgy play of kitschy elements, like the floral Bambi and his domed display of toy ponies.

an urbane array of stripes across the main wall of his living space to give it substance. He saved enough money to buy the antique glass lamp adorned with roses he used to gaze at in the window of a neighborhood lighting shop. "With its roses, it helps express the softer side of my nature," Ruth says, sitting in his otherwise very masculine apartment. "I like that it has thorns, too."

Meanwhile, he started arranging his collection of horns, tusks, taxidermic creatures, and anatomical drawings about his living area, along with his vitrine vignettes. To hide his new bed, he made a screen out of deer netting, casters, and lumber. Since the bed borders a wall of windows, he designed blinds made of two wood frames fitted with translucent plastic slats that

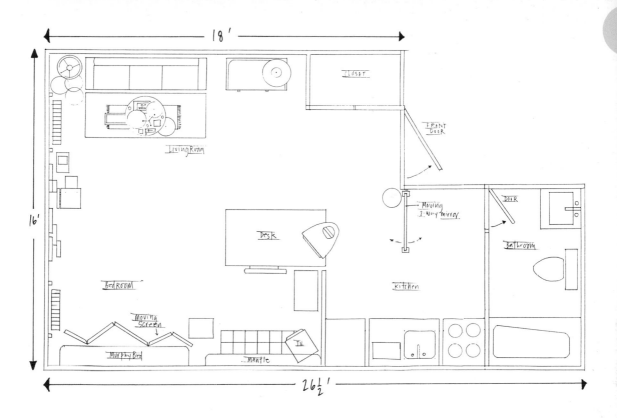

18'

16'

26½'

LivingRoom

CLOSET

FRONT DOOR

Moving 2-Way mirror

DOOR

Bathroom

Desk

Kitchen

BedROOM

Moving Screen

Murphy Bed

Mantle

T.V.

Almost every inch of Ruth's studio is artfully orchestrated, a series of humorously baroque compositions of personal relics, possessions, and passions.

move up and down through a string-and-pulley system. They enable him to look out the window at the midtown skyline without having his neighbors see in. When he wants complete darkness, he pulls down the shades that he sewed together out of brown felt. Ruth has deemed the look "rustic-fancy."

Not long ago, he had a party—his first. Ruth, nevertheless, insists all the effort he went to was for his own pleasure: "I love beauty. And I have exacting standards. So after spending so much time making my home perfect, why not show it off?"

Ruth turned a dinky kitchen into a masculine preserve by painting the metal cabinets brown and adorning those under the counter with strips of silver tape. By fitting inexpensive auto filters over the ceiling spots, he afforded the lights some architectural presence. To shield the bathroom from the rest of the studio, Ruth fashioned a gutsy partition out of a two-way mirror and some lumber appointed with prominent bolts.

A nondescript bathroom became humorous when Ruth made it woodsy, "shingling" the sink's cabinet and adding a wood toilet seat and a shower curtain of wood beads. The painting above the toilet is by Ruth.

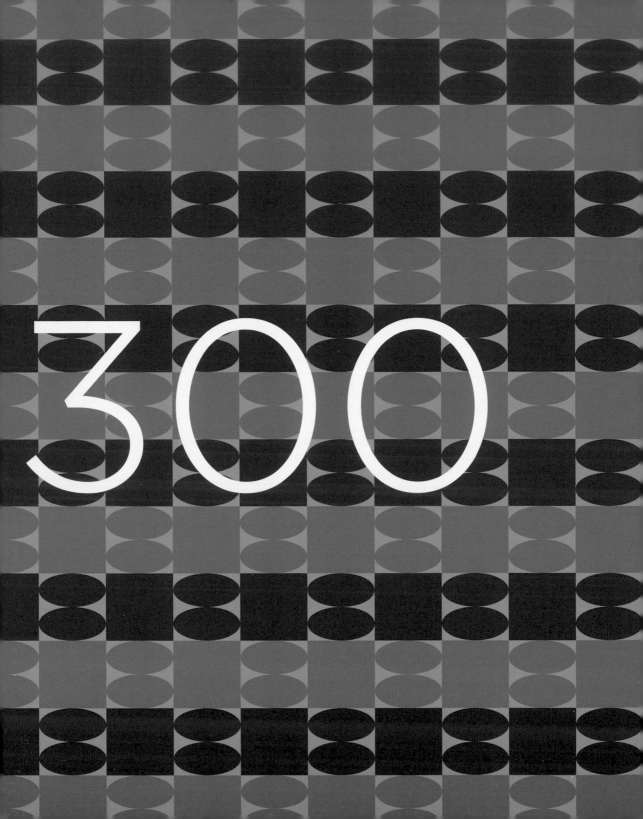

300

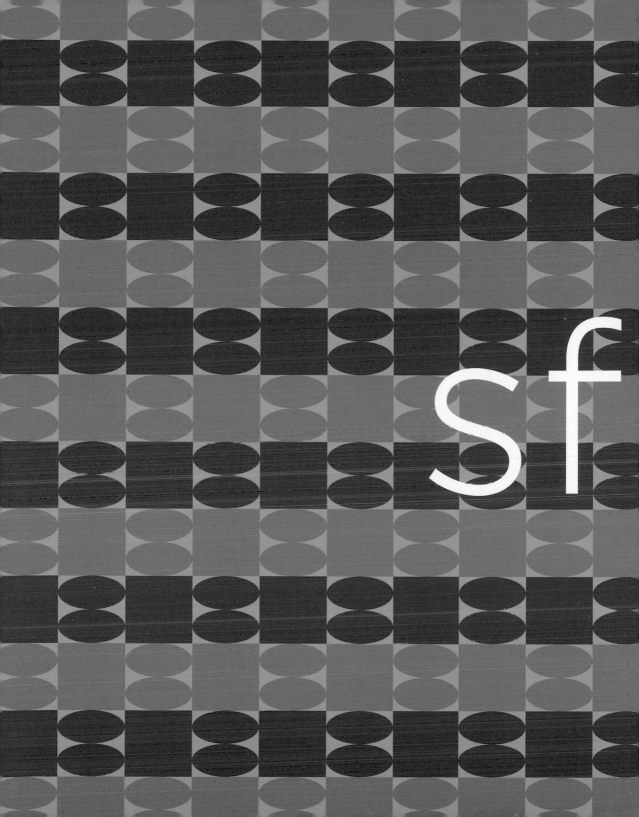

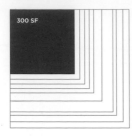

300 SF

CHRISTOPHER COLEMAN

Busy during the week with his work, away to the country on weekends, Christopher Coleman doesn't spend much time at home. He likes to think of his Manhattan studio as a hotel suite, a comfortable place to crash. To be honest, most hotel suites are larger! When Coleman, an interior designer, first moved in eight years ago, he'd just been to Paris and had fallen in love with its many stylish brown interiors. So he decorated his apartment like a formal drawing room in tawny tones. That was when he upholstered the apartment's none-too-even-walls in an ecru cotton twill. (He insists it's much easier to do than you'd think.) After a while, though, he tired of it. He wanted an environment that was more cheerful, more inspiring, more in keeping with his own vibrant self, so he decided to do the whole studio in bright red.

Coleman flaunted design convention when he decorated his Lilliputian pad in fire-engine red. The effect is cheerfully electric.

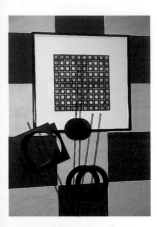

A red-and-white check wallpaper distinguishes the kitchen from the living area, while giving it some jaunty life.

A sideboard—on wheels, like most of the apartment's furnishings—makes up for the kitchen's minimal storage space.

Bright red in a small space? Yes, and with checkerboard walls, too! Once Coleman decided on a color, he set about devising a new layout. He's always emphasizing to clients how important such planning is. It's a great aid when figuring out the flow and scale for a room. Previously, when the studio resembled a drawing room, he had slept on a daybed. Now he felt more comfortable with the studio being a straightforward bedroom, so he decided on a full-size bed, centrally situated. All the room's other furniture and activities had to conform to this one piece. As Coleman desired a little corner for working and relaxing, he designed a diminutive loveseat upholstered in red

By putting the studio's corners to use for storage, Coleman was able to keep the apartment's walls uncluttered, enhancing its sense of openness.

Exchanging closet doors for draperies, Coleman softened the rigorous geometries of the foyer.

leather. He searched everywhere before he found a work/dining table to go with it. Like almost all the other furnishings in the apartment, he wanted it be small-scaled and on wheels. The Battista table that he selected is also collapsible. Coleman designed just about everything else: the canister poufs; the red acrylic bed stands that double as cupboards; and the low stainless-steel console that holds the television and magazines. Believing that there's no such thing as too much closet space, he installed extra closets on either side of his bed, hiding them behind red draperies so they would blend in with the window treatment.

Coleman framed his bed with red curtains, adding drama while concealing storage. His red acrylic nightstands also serve as mini wardrobes.

Coleman covered the walls of the entry and kitchen with a red checkerboard wallpaper to distinguish this service area from the rest of the apartment. The bold pattern injects some jaunty life into the otherwise unremark-
able space. To soften the sharp lines, he replaced the closet doors with the
same heavy red curtains he used by the bed. Through his skilled balancing
of hard and soft geometries throughout the studio, Coleman has pulled off
a decorative mission impossible: he's created a high-voltage, high-drama
environment that also happens to be inviting and cozy. Is it any wonder his
services are so in demand?

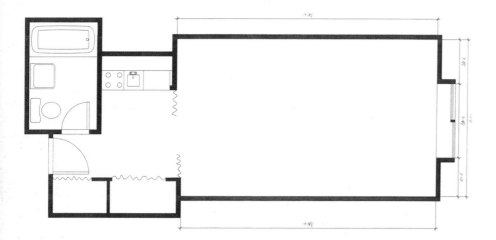

300 SF

JORGE VARGAS

Step into Jorge Vargas's apartment and you know you're in the home of someone who has spent a life in the theater. Because it's about drama, baby, drama. Vargas was for many years a ballet dancer, "a gypsy who traveled the world," he says, in an appropriately world-weary voice. A dancer's life is short. When the curtain came down on his career, Vargas moved to Miami and became a makeup artist. He was there for nine years before Broadway

Flamboyant, yes, but what personality for a postwar flat! A fearless use of brilliant color, lively pattern, and architectural detail packs a visual punch.

The studio's Corinthian columns (blow-ups from a Piranesi etching) give it height and authority. A collection of curvy furnishings—the circular mirror in a frame composed of myriad aluminum pull tops, the sofa with a crescent cut-out, and the egg-shaped chair—all soften the edges of the boxy room.

beckoned with the offer of a long-term gig as makeup supervisor for the musical *Aida*, and Vargas jetéd at the chance. He sold his furniture and headed north with just two suitcases. "I made a complete break," he says. "It was frightening and exhilarating at once." The Manhattan rental he found was sleek and well situated, but a mere 300 square feet. What to do? "I have many skills, but home decorating is not one of them," he admits. He called one of his oldest, dearest friends, a former-dancer-turned-interior-designer, Matthew White.

Although he's used to working on a more palatial scale, White was tickled by the prospect of designing a little home for an old friend on the brink of a new life. Other than requesting a sofabed and "a touch of animal," Vargas gave him carte blanche. The first thing White thought about was color. "Jorge had always lived in white spaces, and they never seemed suited to him. Because he's a makeup artist, I wanted the room to be painted a color flattering to skin tone." Before long, White sent Vargas a bright orange color swatch, with a note asking: "Can you live with this?" It was "the color of the papayas I used to eat as a boy in Colombia," Vargas says. "This was so radical. I was thrilled." He immediately set about "auditioning" painters.

Meanwhile, the Pasadena, California–based White went hunting for fun, splashy props at off-Broadway prices in thrift shops and flea markets. When he snagged a knockoff of the Eero Aarnio Ball chair, he had his scenic

anchor. He would enliven Vargas's new stage set with a twist of 1960s fanta-sia. To give the boxy room an architectural dimension, White filched some columns from an eighteenth-century engraving, color-copied them, and then enlarged them till they were ten feet tall. Playing further upon a classi-cal theme, he enlarged a small Piranesi engraving to nearly seven feet high and had it framed, and ordered the manufacture of a small Ionic capital to serve as a television stand. He designed the cartoonish curved-back sofabed, and from his friend, artist Clare Graham, a mistress of recycling, he commissioned a circular mirror framed with 17,000 pull tops to place above it. For that "touch of animal," he bought a white-tiger carpet off the bolt and bound it in flame-red carpeting. "Very Siegfried & Roy," says Vargas with a throaty laugh.

On a Wednesday, when Vargas was away all day because of the matinee performance, White and a helper flew in and put the whole apartment together. When Vargas returned late that evening, it was as if the curtain went up. The set for his new life was complete. Happily, the design, like *Aida*, has had legs. "I appreciate it more and more every day," says Vargas. Friends are so enamored with "the Papaya," they clamor for him to give parties, offering to bring the food themselves. Vargas is happy to comply. "For years I was a good guest, now I'm a good host." What pleases him most, says Vargas, is that when guests come over, "everybody looks good everywhere."

The studio was designed to have a 1960s Pop flair. Pol-ished as the look is, it was achieved without much expense. The egg chair is from a flea market; other furnishings came from thrift shops. But the studio also features some singular details, like the HVAC-cover crafted from old aluminum can tops and the window coverings made of metal beading, both by Clare Graham.

This little wood chair may play only a supporting role in the studio's decor, but its exceptional form—it's as lithe as a dancer—contributes to the studio's rich detail.

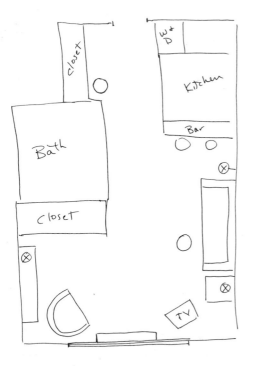

Black-and-white and silver motifs make urbane counterpoints to the studio's panoply of vivid colors.

In the apartment's entry, Graham assembled a Memphis-like sculpture out of colorful plastic serving ware.

350

350 SF

WILLIAM STEWART AND JOHN DYER

William Stewart and John Dyer live and work in Atlanta, but they love Manhattan. Culture mavens, they relish the city's myriad attractions, especially its galleries and restaurants. Both Stewart and Dyer work in the design world, so when they thought about getting their own pied-à-terre, they were thinking of something with exceptional architectural character. Instead, by a fluke, they ended up with a 350-square-foot postwar studio. It had "no view, no light, no distinctive details, and zero romance. It was

A mix of pedigree Modern furnishings, African masks and stools, and sculptural ceramics bring detail and distinction to an otherwise undistinguished postwar studio.

absolutely plain vanilla when I found it," says Stewart. "But what it does have is location." It's in the heart of Manhattan's Greenwich Village.

The pair weren't interested in spending a great deal of time and imagination decorating the place, even though it was clearly in need of help. They wanted to be out enjoying the city. What's more, they were already in the midst of remodeling their house in Atlanta and furnishing it with the best works of mid-century Modernism they could scout. Because they didn't know how long their love affair with Manhattan might last, when selecting furniture the two decided to think of their studio as an extension of their home. If they gave up the lease, their pieces could always migrate south.

With some clever design thinking and some exceptional furnishings, the two created a casual but sophisticated urban oasis. Stewart began the project by painting the space a cheery chartreuse. Annoyed by a strangely located column in the entry, he splashed some black paint on it "to make it look like an I-beam." In doing so, he fortuitously gave the apartment an architectural

By painting a structural column black, Stewart transformed an eyesore into an architectural feature. The chartreuse-hued walls bring some visual zing to a studio with little natural light.

As it's used mostly as a weekend pied-á-terre, the studio has a loungey feel. A double bed covered in a sumptuous brown chenille makes for cozy seating. The low coffee table and the flokati rug invite guests to stretch out on the floor. The lattice work of Jean Royére's elaborate sconce adds some needed detail to the boxy room, as do the African masks.

exclamation. A wonderful lattice sconce by Jean Royère, purchased later, adds some more detailing to the boxlike room.

Instead of going the sofabed route, Stewart bought a full-size bed, placing it against the wall and decorating it with a custom bedcover and some throw pillows. The loungey effect was exactly what he was after. "This is a place to hang out at after a day on the town, to read magazines and listen to music," he explains. The only entertaining would be occasionally having a few friends over for some white wine and cheese. "The city would be our living and

A toy robot possesses a totemic quality much like the studio's African masks. A biomorphic sconce by Georges Jouve softens the studio's sharp geometries.

dining room," says Stewart. The couple purchased a fabulous Royère side-board for the apartment, which with its iron grillwork endows the room with even more detail, in addition to a low coffee table by Jean Prouvé and Charlotte Perriand. They didn't install any track or overhead lighting, but relied on very simple sconces and table lamps, placed at different levels about the room to give it a soft ambience. They threw a shag rug on the floor to encourage stretching out. As Stewart points out, the studio doesn't have high ceilings, so the lower you sit, the more spacious it feels.

Avid art collectors, Dyer and Stewart's next goal was to find the right pieces for the walls. A weekend trip to the Chelsea flea market yielded a host of inexpensive African masks that engage the modern furnishings in a lively dialogue. Two months after they got their lease, in just a few weekend visits, the apartment was complete. It's been such a success they no longer think about packing things up and moving them to Atlanta. Instead, they're con-sidering finding a bigger New York City apartment.

John Dyer (left) and
William Stewart

400

JUDY HUDSON AND STUART BASSECHES

About ten years ago, when Stuart Basseches moved into his 400-square-foot one-bedroom in Manhattan's Flatiron District, the neighborhood was not nearly as glamorous as it is today, and the apartment was undeniably shabby. But it was cheap and the big windows walling the living area made it wonderfully open. Being an architect, Basseches wanted to give the simple layout some surprise, so he built an L-shaped wall to partially obscure the urban vistas of the living area from the entry. That wall also became the support for a coat closet, which he constructed on the entry side, and for

Crisply tailored furnishings in zesty tones, most from the couple's company Biproduct, make a tiny living room look sharp.

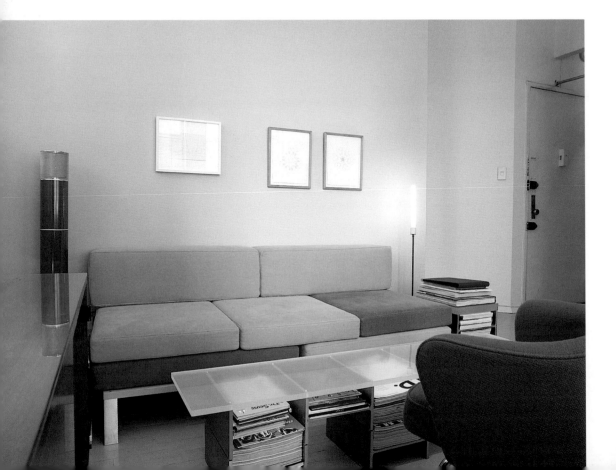

the extra kitchen cabinets and counterspace that he installed on the other. To better illumine the space, he ran some low-voltage lighting of his own design from the ceiling and added a host of his signature table lamps. "Lots of lighting activity keeps your eyes moving about the room, so they don't focus on one point," says Basseches, "so the room feels bigger."

Such is the nature of New York City life that a few years later when his future wife, Judy Hudson, first saw his apartment she was almost as taken

Basseches' coffee and side tables are smartly designed to store a library's worth of magazines. A scattering of low-voltage lights keeps the eye moving about the room, making it feel bigger.

A mirrored door brightens and expands a small bathroom. Bits of color and an over-sized light bulb animate the room.

with it as with him. "My apartment was *really* small," she says. "There were *no* closets." When Hudson moved in, color came into Basseches' surroundings: together they painted the kitchen wall a bright orange. Love turned into marriage, and an inspired Basseches decided to set up a furniture company, making products that combined industrial materials and bright colors.

To transform the apartment into an efficient home-office for his new endeavor, he crafted a long wood slab and inserted it along one of the living room's windowed walls. The wood shelf became worktop and dining table.

Basseches added a wall by the entry when he moved in, which created a small alcove between the living room and kitchen. He installed on the kitchen side shelves and a cabinet to improve on the tiny kitchen's limited storage. When he and his wife had a baby, the alcove became the baby's room, right, with the simple, ingenious addition of an acrylic partition and felt curtains. What was once the bar area, now serves as the diaper station.

So pleasing was Basseches' work situation that Hudson, a graphic designer, set up her office at the other end of the countertop. The quarters were tight, but the couple flourished, in part because they were disciplined about maintaining the clarity of the space. Every so often they purge quotidian detritus. Superfluous furnishings and materials are banished to storage; books are pared down to their favorite ten. What then remains, says Hudson, are those objects most charged with meaning, personality, and pleasure—like the vintage black globe in the living room that was Basseches' first birthday present to Hudson. "The apartment," she says, "doesn't feel minimalist at all."

If they eliminated stuff, they welcomed color. The couple painted the living room wall a dove gray and the bedroom a light chartreuse. Basseches designed a sofa with upholstered cushions in saffron and olive. The pair

chanced upon some Eero Saarinen-designed armchairs and reupholstered them in a tangerine-colored fabric, the same hue as Basseches' newly designed table lamp. The more brilliant the colors were that animated their surroundings, the happier they felt in them.

Next, Ivy appeared. Not a greenish hue, but a baby daughter. The apartment went through yet another transformation. Basseches sliced away part of the worktop (the couple did eventually rent an office) in order to make a feeding station. In the kitchen alcove, he created a room within a room for Ivy by installing an acrylic partition wall directly in front of the kitchen and hanging industrial bleached-felt "curtains" from rollers in front of the partition and the alcove's entry.

Opposite, when the felt curtain is rolled down the kitchen disappears from view. Bottom, the alcove is insulated from the noise and light of the street and the living room when the exterior curtains are down. The wood counter extends to the far end of the apartment, serving as worktop and dining table.

With merry ingenuity, Basseches and Hudson have made their tiny apartment livable for their new family for now. When Ivy gets older, of course,
they know they will have to move to a larger home. "Twelve hundred square
feet would probably be sufficient," muses Basseches. Almost three times
the size of their current residence, that figure sounds palatial.

It doesn't take much to make
a stylish room. A colorfully
checkered blanket pulls
together all of the bedroom's
disparate, brightly hued
elements.

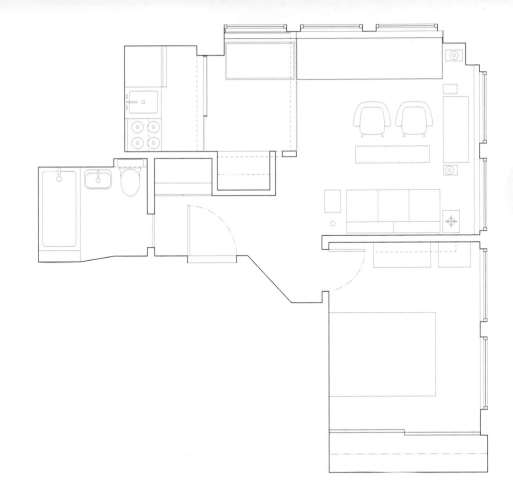

400 SF

STEPHEN EARLE

Stephen Earle, the home director of Martha Stewart Omnimedia, recognized "a good thing" when he first glimpsed his studio in Manhattan's Chelsea. "It was just what I wanted, one square, pleasantly shaped room," he says. "And there was an alcove for a Murphy bed." He had long ago been converted to the joys and efficiencies of these space savers. Earle didn't need much space, though. He had recently bought a second weekend house, so a pied-à-terre was all he required for his Manhattan digs. "It's my idealized hotel room," says Earle. "I keep only what I need here."

This studio brims with pedigreed furniture and *objets,* but because the pieces are light in line and hue, the room still feels airy and casual.

For Earle, keeping things spare and functional is the key to one-room living. This meant renovating the minuscule kitchen and eliminating much that was in it. "It was comical," he says. "It had full-size appliances and about one square inch of counter space!" As his weekday cooking is minimal at best, he installed only two burners, a below-counter fridge, and a microwave. There's no oven. Now he has plenty of counter space for what little meal preparation he does.

The space looks more like a salon than a studio apartment thanks to Earle's clever mix of pedigree furnishings, flea market finds, and utilitarian basics. Among the furnishings are works by Charles and Ray Eames, George Nelson, Diego Giacometti, Jean Prouvé, Florence Knoll, and potter Barbara Willis. It also features twin black utility cabinets for extra storage: their color and scale give them an unexpected elegance. The Thebes stools that stand on top like ornaments on a pediment add to the lockers' architectural allure and turn out to be a smart way to store additional seating. For a small room,

Utility lockers, above, compensate for limited closet space. Positioned like twin sentries by the living room's entry, the spare, black forms take on an architectural presence, while the antique Thebes stools, stored on top, give them a classical twist. A long row of Shakeresque clothing hooks, opposite, maximize the function of the little entry hall, as does the small shelf balanced above the moldings where sweaters are neatly stored in lightweight bins. A retro chandelier and rich brown walls give the foyer a masculine elegance.

Earle has filled it with a lot of furniture, but because of lean lines and neutral tones of the pieces, and the mix of geometries, the eye dances around the space and never feels confined. In turn, Earle's collection of pale-toned ceramics has a unifying effect.

Like all highly functional small spaces, many of the furnishings do double duty. A square side table that stands against the wall can be pulled out into the room and set for four. (Most of the time, though, when Earle entertains, friends eat buffet-style around the Herman Miller coffee table.) The red chest opens to reveal a small writing desk. And adjacent to it, hidden behind the narrow white blind, is a filing cabinet and stored office supplies. The larger white blind hides Earle's "secret bedroom." If Earle is almost evangelical in his appreciation for Murphy beds, it's because they work a kind of spatial magic: "Often I'll be in my bed and I'll look around the room, and realize I have a much bigger—and nicer—bedroom than most New Yorkers." It's one that becomes an equally lovely living room by day!

Below, inexpensive rolling shades camouflage the Murphy-bed closet and the niche where a file cabinet and office equipment are stored. The bittersweet-hued George Nelson-designed chest contains a drop-front desk.

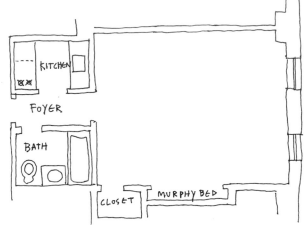

KITCHEN

FOYER

BATH

CLOSET   MURPHY BED

As the studio serves only as a weekday home, Earle renovated the tiny kitchen for minimal cooking: he installed a microwave (instead of an oven) and a space-saving two-burner stove. As he does entertain, usually serving take-out, he added a full-size dishwasher. While he splurged on a Corian countertop, he chose cabinets from Ikea.

400 SF

VIRGINIA BRIGGS

A subscription to the *New Yorker* first conjured dreams of big-city life in Virginia Briggs when she was a college freshman. Sixty years later, the retired psychologist finally made the move, joining her two daughters and grandchildren on Manhattan's Upper West Side. Leaving her native southern California involved certain domestic sacrifices, namely, space and newness. "Things fall down there before they get old," she notes wryly. But Briggs found a neat compromise: a sunny, ground-floor alcove studio in a sleek apartment building, with a big picture window looking out onto open, prettily landscaped grounds—about as close to California living as a New Yorker can get.

When Briggs downsized from a big house to an alcove studio, she brought along some major pieces of furniture. While imposing, they define the space and provide lots of storage.

But her new home was only 400 square feet. Her previous house had been more than five times as big. She still had the furniture to prove it. While she disposed of much, she surprisingly was able to keep some of the largest pieces, thanks to the spatial ingenuity of her daughter Claire, who helped her organize the apartment. Together they lined the studio's long, narrow hall—typically dead space—with a breakfront and an étagère, which have narrow footprints but accommodate a generous treasure trove of family photos, keepsakes, and tchotchkes.

They also arranged an armoire, a desk, some wood file cabinets, and a shoji screen to make a distinct office space with lots of storage for Briggs's copious files from her former research. The clever layout enables her to enjoy the view from her window while working at her computer, or to close off the space with the shoji screen when she's not.

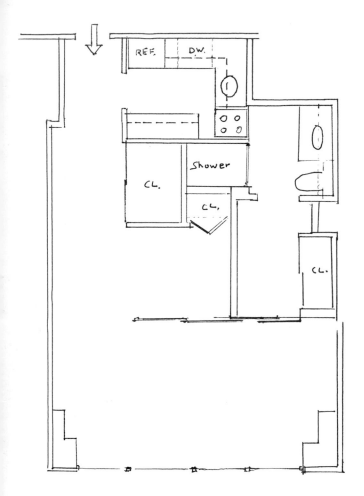

A wall of windows with a garden view keeps this generously furnished apartment from feeling cramped. A shoji screen divides the little office from the rest of studio. When the panel is slid back, Briggs can be at her desk and still enjoy the view.

Furniture lines the walls of the rest of the living space. Close to her beloved La-Z-Boy lounger, where Briggs often sits while catching up on the latest psychology journals, there's her piano, a loveseat, and her Murphy bed, which is an unusual version that folds out horizontally, taking up only the bottom half of the wall. It's a lot of furniture, mostly big pieces, but easy circulation within the space and a wide window, connecting the room to the open landscape outside, make the studio feel airy and appealing. A mirror above the Murphy bed only enhances the sense of openness.

Adapting to city life was arduous at first for Briggs; she had a hard time adjusting to not driving. A music lover, she has, however, gotten used to walking the few short blocks from her home to concerts at Lincoln Center. "I'm beginning to feel like a New Yorker," says Briggs with a gleam in her eye worthy of a college freshman.

The mirrored wall gives the room an expansive ambiance. Under the large mirror is the twin-sized Murphy bed. By lining her furniture along the studio's walls, Briggs was able to maximize its limited space, while allowing for easy movement throughout.

450

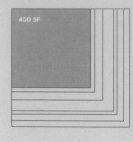

450 SF

LESLIE HOFFMAN

When Leslie Hoffman first arrived in New York City to head an environmental foundation, she lived in a spacious, sunny loft in the Tribeca section of lower Manhattan. But her office was in midtown, and it's there she spent her days and sometimes evenings. So after a time, she decided to move nearer to her work. She targeted an Upper East Side neighborhood, full of charming brownstones and a stone's throw from Central Park. But it was pricey. Finally, she chanced upon an affordable, if dinky, one-bedroom. Dark and narrow, its attraction for Hoffman was a working fireplace and a terrace just big enough for sunning and pot gardening. A couple of years later, the

Hoffman's alterations to her flat include this window, which she had punched out to obtain more light and extra lounging and storage space via the built-in window seat. A television and sound system are hidden in the armoire.

Hoffman added a side door
to her ample walk-in closet
so it could do double duty
as a coat closet.

building went co-op, and Hoffman planned to move on. But when the deal
on a new dream apartment fell through, she was too depressed to look further. She bought her apartment determined to pull it apart and put it
together in a more livable way.

"I spent every free moment thinking about how I could do it," recalls Hoffman, whose first career was as a designer–builder in Maine. "I sketched and
I measured. I asked everyone for their suggestions." She knew she wanted
more light, a walk-in closet, a kitchen with a dishwasher and a full-size stove,
a Jacuzzi, and a washer/dryer. The question was how to get all that into a
450-square-foot space without the walls closing in. The answer came from
the suggestions of two friends. One proposed knocking out the existing
window and back wall, and building a large bay window with a seat to afford
the living area more light and a sense of openness. The other told her to
get rid of the dividing bedroom wall and buy a newfangled bed system in
which the bed is stored in the ceiling—yes, ceiling—and electronically lowers
on pulleys.

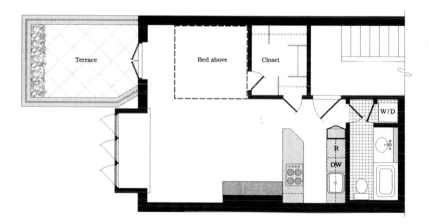

She took their suggestions. Where her bed had once stood, Hoffman constructed a desk and dresser unit and installed the bed system above it. At night, she lowers the bed down on top of the dresser unit and then uses her desk chair, which flips into a stepping stool, to climb aboard. The space where a Murphy bed might have been stored is now part of Hoffman's walk-in closet. Scrupulous about maximizing every square inch of space, she cut out another doorway into the closet from the main living area so it could do double duty as a coat closet. Hoffman's spatial ingenuity enabled her to carve out enough space for a luxurious bathroom and a laundry area.

When an apartment is this compact, even a tiny kitchen takes on a major presence. As Hoffman's kitchen was essentially in her living room, she selected cabinets crafted out of solid bird's-eye maple with walnut beading

Here, the work and sleeping spaces are the same, thanks to a nifty system that hides the bed in the ceiling. Hoffman's desk chair converts into a step ladder when she wants to ascend to the land of nod.

As Hoffman's kitchen is literally in her living room, she chose cabinetry that would resemble furniture. An extra-skinny refrigerator leaves space for more storage cabinets.

The bathroom is narrow but long, accommodating a generously sized bath and sink. There's also a small washer/dryer unit.

A terrace, large enough for a
pot garden, contributes to
the apartment's pleasure.

so they would look like "fancy furniture." Other than some pretty antique
French fruitwood dining chairs and a Southeast Asian wood table, the only
furniture in the apartment is a loveseat and ottoman, a Japanese cabinet,
and an armoire, which houses her stereo and television.

That's all she needs. Since Hoffman spends her weekends in the country, she
considers her apartment a solitary retreat from the stresses of the working
week. "I don't keep my books here, I don't even get mail," she says, explaining one of her stratagems for reducing the clutter in her little home. "When
I'm here, I'm listening to music or catching the news before I go to bed. I
don't have to worry about anything else."

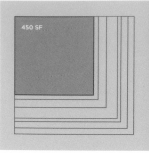

450 SF

MARY TRASKO

Most young urbanites see studio apartments as stepping-stones to larger homes. When Mary Trasko found her Chelsea studio, this sense of temporariness was compounded by the fact that the apartment was a sublet. She thought she'd be lucky if she could stay two years. Some eighteen years later, she's still here. More remarkable, perhaps, she discovered over the years that her little nest possesses everything she desires.

Most studios with Murphy beds masquerade as living rooms. Here, the studio is unabashedly a boudoir.

The light is what she loves most. During the day, the apartment glows. Two windows in the living area and one in the kitchen afford big views of the sky, enhancing the studio's airiness. "I never feel as if I'm living in a small room," she observes. And it's this strong sense of openness that has enabled her to ignore just about all the decorating caveats for a small space. Most strikingly, there's little uniformity to the decor. Rather than having a formal plan, Trasko, a writer and publicist for a shoe company, has decorated through impulse and accretion. The objects and artworks that adorn the walls and surfaces have been picked up during her journeys—she travels widely and often—or, like the two large paintings that hang on the long wall, acquired from artist friends. Most design authorities warn that works of so large a scale will overpower a small room. But here they ground it and are in turn balanced by the smaller artworks on the other walls and the intriguing collections of shells, ornate glasses, and porcelain in the vitrine. The

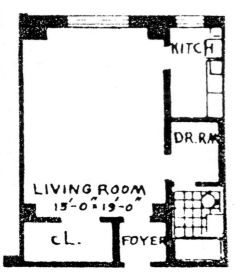

Trasko's apartment is a mix of patterns, colors, and collections. What they share is a certain sprightliness and delicacy of form.

When Trasko gives a party,
she slips her bed into its closet alcove. In this open space
she's held elaborate costume
parties for as many as seventy
guests, with lots of dancing,
even the occasional Conga.

large mirror contributes by providing the space with a more open feel. Dispensing with design theory, Trasko goes to the heart of the room's appeal: "What could be more glorious than waking up every morning and seeing this gorgeous horse galloping through your room?"

Trasko has never found the limited square footage to be an impediment to any of her homebound pursuits. She's written several books here, though more often on her bed than at her desk. She also entertains. For many years she gave a fabled annual costume party in which more than seventy people might show up over the course of the evening, and the dancing would go well into the night. (Think Holly Golightly's party in *Breakfast at Tiffany's*.) Her strategy for throwing a big bash in such a little space was simple: lots of plastic cups and a bathtub overflowing with ice and champagne. Cooking has never held any interest for her. Now that she prefers more intimate gatherings, she invites guests over for hors d'oeuvres and Prosecco. Most times Trasko doesn't bother to put away her bed. If eighteenth-century aristocrats could entertain guests and dine in their boudoirs, why can't she?

In decorating her studio, Trasko broke many set rules of small space design. Two oversized paintings dominate the main wall, and there's a happy clutter of pretty objects.

Life for Trasko is indeed a moveable feast, which may be why she has no intention of ever pulling up stakes. "Living in a small space is very freeing," she says. "There are very few things to weigh you down. You have no big responsibilities, so you can just lock the door and go." There is, however, a certain discipline required in maintaining some spatial austerity. "My relationship to things is always in a kind of flow," notes Trasko. "Recently I bought a new painting, and I got rid of a couple of chairs. I purge the apartment of some possessions about every six months, so the space is always changing." She declares she doesn't feel very attached to things, but then revises that thought. "I can't imagine ever getting rid of any of my art, or for that matter my forty pairs of Roger Vivier shoes." But then as any collector of vintage shoes will attest, they, too, are works of art.

450 SF

DONALD ALBRECHT

Donald Albrecht has three great loves: architecture, film, and New York City. In his studio, they all live happily together. When Albrecht, an architecture and design curator, went apartment hunting fifteen years ago, he didn't have much money to spend, but he knew what he wanted: an apartment with architectural character, in the kind of classic Manhattan neighborhood favored by the silver screen. What he found was a grimy studio that hadn't been painted for some thirty years! However, it had a sunken living room

It's the furniture in this bi-level studio that defines its different zones of activity. Though the pieces come from various modern periods, they make convivial companions, thanks to the harmony of their lines and forms.

By adding a short partition of double-faced book shelves, Albrecht was able to divide his studio into two distinct rooms. Below, the glazed bookshelves are recessed in what had been an alcove for a Murphy bed. Albrecht sleeps instead on a trundle that doubles as a day bed.

and a nifty dressing compartment. It was in a fabulous Gothic-Deco building, designed by one of the city's forgotten architectural visionaries, Harvey Wiley Corbett. Its swank lobby with baronial wood paneling and silver chandeliers looked like a set from Metro Goldwyn Mayer's 1936 comedy classic *My Man Godfrey*. And it was situated in the heart of midtown, as classic as Manhattan neighborhoods get. (To see another treatment of an identical floor plan, see page 140.)

Albrecht was working at home a lot, so he consulted with an architect friend, Louis Poupon, about how best to organize the studio as a living/

working space. Poupon suggested he turn the large foyer, where the apartment's original Murphy bed was located, into a work area and then combine his sleeping and living arrangements on the lower level. The plan made tremendous sense, but Albrecht couldn't imagine spending his days sitting so far away from the studio's windows. He wanted a view when he toiled at his desk, so he decided to keep the bed where it was. Then there was the issue of his books—he had quite a collection. Albrecht needed lots of shelving, but he didn't want his studio to resemble a library. Where a spindly rail had set off the division between the studio's two levels, Poupon designed double-faced bookshelves that, by definitively separating the apartment's sections, while still leaving the room open, read more as architecture than book storage. "Spatial boundaries that are porous" says Albrecht, who trained as an architect, ". . . it's a lesson right out of John Soane."

Albrecht placed his desk in the corner by the window, so he could enjoy the view. Equipped with plenty of storage, it can be in full view without being a messy eyesore.

As Albrecht had more books than clothes, he turned part of his efficiently designed dressing closet into a library.

Poupon ripped out the Murphy bed and installed more bookshelves in its former closet, which he encased in glass. Below them, he inserted a trundle bed. Transformed into a cozy reading nook, the foyer now seemed a more inviting place to sleep. The spillover of tomes was tucked away in the small but surprisingly spacious dressing area.

To give the apartment added architectural distinction, Albrecht painted the walls a light celadon and the doors and moldings a darker tone of green. For furnishings, he chose pieces that he felt evoked the Modernism of the 1930s, '40s, and '50s, close to the era of his building. He nods at his Venetian-style mirror and laughs, saying, "Eventually, I got tired of being a Modernist." But even that bit of overscaled opulence, he argues, is in keeping with the 1930s, especially in regard to the films of that era. "They called the look Hollywood Regency. Remember the glamorous sets of the Astaire–Rogers movies?" Indeed.

Albrecht's sunlit galley kitchen, a 1930s classic, may be small, but it's efficient. He often cooks for friends.

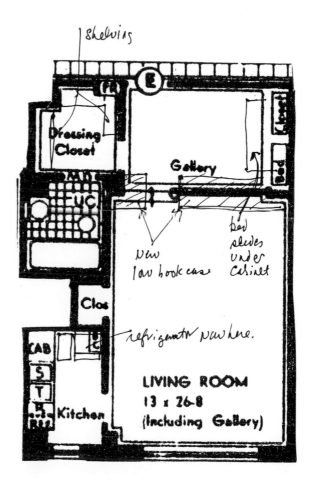

137

The delights of Albrecht's apartment are inside and out: a favorite Bertoia chair, and a favorite view—the Empire State Building.

450 SF

FRANCISCO PARDO AND XIMENA OROZCO

When Francisco Pardo and Ximena Orozco, two young architects, came to Manhattan from Mexico City to pursue their architectural careers, they set up shop and housekeeping in a 450-square-foot studio apartment in midtown. Its trim rectangular shape and rationalized layout appealed to them. "It has a separate balcony gallery for a bed, and all the service components—the kitchen, bathroom, dressing alcove—are arranged on one side," says Pardo approvingly. "How very architectural of you to note that," interjects his wife.

Pardo and Orozco knew they wouldn't be in the city forever; their hearts belong to Mexico. There wasn't any point investing lots of time or money in a dramatic intervention, so they made only the most elemental additions.

Minimal furnishings and a monochromatic color scheme enhance the spacious feel of this studio, which is a necessity given that this home is also a workspace.

They designed a clean-lined blond wood closet for their Murphy bed with shelves on each side for books, a clock, and a water glass, all of which are hidden when the bed's closet doors are closed. "When the bed is folded away, the unit blends in with the wall," says Orozco. "Friends who have come over to see the apartment always say as they're leaving, 'We never got to see your bedroom.' 'You're standing in it,' we tell them." In the dressing room, the couple also built a Bauhausian grid of plastic bins to store their clothes and other personal items.

What the couple wanted most was an apartment that felt spacious and airy, since it needed to serve as both home and office. To achieve this they painted the apartment a bright Modernist white, and lined their furniture against the walls. Almost all of it is from Ikea—good bones at affordable prices. One modest shelving unit serves as both office and life organizer, housing their sleek IBM workstation, their scanner, printer, and fax, along with their modest collection of books, CDs, and their neatly boxed work archives.

A blond wood cabinet, designed by the couple, houses their Murphy bed. It blends seamlessly into the simple decor, enhancing its sense of airiness and light.

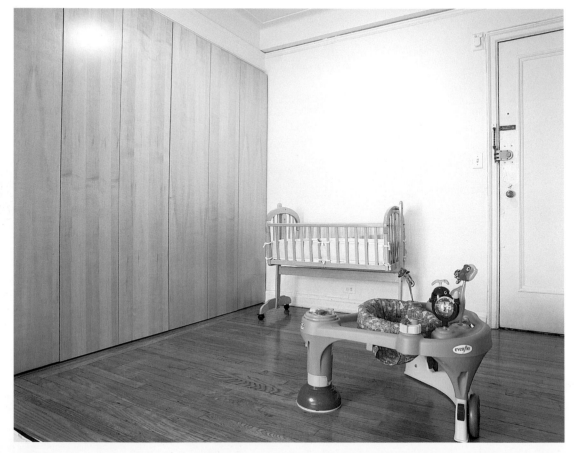

Sliding bins in a wood grid serve as clothes storage in the dressing alcove.

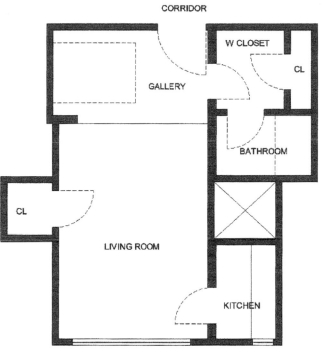

CORRIDOR

W CLOSET

CL

GALLERY

BATHROOM

CL

LIVING ROOM

KITCHEN

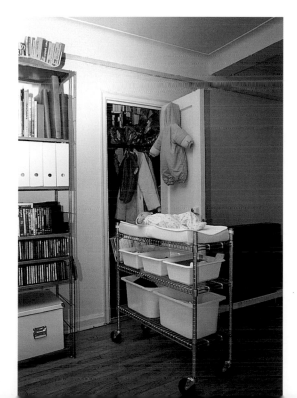

A deep closet holds the baby's diaper station as well as coats.

Being architects, they're disciplined about organization, keeping everything precisely in its place. The walls are mostly bare. "We don't have a lot of stuff showing. Most people want to fill spaces with pictures they don't really need," observes Pardo. "Openness," he says, "is the pleasure of this place." There are some photographs on display, though, mostly of the couple. Even minimalism has its personal side.

When a big, beautiful, bouncy baby named Francisca arrived on the scene, the couple made a few more additions. They bought a simple blond wood crib, and made a wheeled shelving unit into a diaper station, which they store in the coat closet. The open sleeping level serves as Francisca's play area. Carefully conceived interiors, especially small ones, are typically thrown into chaos by the arrival of a baby, but Pardo and Orozco have managed to preserve the spare serenity they so cherish in their apartment. One might call it a triumph of minimalist living.

A single hanging light defines the dining area; two Eames chairs give the room design distinction. When a space is this simply furnished, a solitary object, even something as small as this whimsical salt-and-pepper shaker, can become a decorative accent.

500

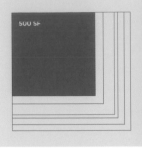

500 SF

ISABELLE BOSQUET

Isabelle Bosquet found her little gem of an apartment atop a six-floor walk-up in the heart of Manhattan's Greenwich Village. Its quirky layout immediately appealed to her. The narrow rooms snake around the building, providing surprising spatial intrigue and a flood of daylight and urban views through the many windows. The apartment, however, had a big drawback. The building was at the start of a long, dusty, noisy renovation. Bosquet

The intrepid use of red and other brilliant hues brings an exotic sumptuousness to this one bedroom.

decided to endure, excited by the opportunity to have a say in the apartment's refurbishment. A floral designer, she had been camping out for a long time in her work studio—a big, stunning space, but one lacking in homely amenities. With working days that begin early, end late, and encompass a whirl of activities, she needed a quiet haven where she could read, relax, listen to music, and occasionally entertain. So determined was she to conjure domestic tranquility in her new home that she banned television and telephone. (She does carry a cell phone.)

Few design experts would have concurred with Bosquet that a scarlet red decor conjures serenity. Yet here it seems to work. Rather than overwhelm, the red furnishings and accessories, interwoven with other colors

The wall's simple red stencils, painted by Bosquet, contribute to the apartment's decorative richness.

An assortment of red objects in various forms gives depth to Bosquet's design statement.

and balanced by white walls, ground and unite the rooms, imbuing them with sociable and sumptuous warmth. The decor's vibrancy and drama harmonizes, too, with Bosquet's own Amazonian vibe. Almost six feet tall, she is famously energetic, independent, and fearless, often traveling alone to far-flung, exotic lands. Most of the apartment's wall hangings, lamps, rugs, and other *objets* were picked up during her trips through Central America and Asia and in the souks and bazaars of Morocco and Turkey. The apartment's other basics—the bookcase, the sofa, the dressers, the bed frame—come from that great motherland of affordable design, Ikea.

As she only occasionally has dinner guests, Bosquet doesn't need a big dining table. To save space, she uses a desk, the top of which opens to seat four.

Since there seems to be a drop or two of the nomadic Bedouin in Bosquet's blood, there's no telling how long she'll stay anywhere. The beauty of her little retreat is that its most vivid elements are all easily transportable. The colorful rugs that adorn the floors and walls just need to be rolled up. The brightly patterned Turkish border tiles that enliven the kitchen can be easily peeled off, since she adhered them to the walls with double-sided tape. Right now, though, Bosquet has no plans to go anywhere. She has a hard time imagining a more delightful city home. At night, the last thing she sees out her bedroom window before closing her eyes is the fancifully lit form of the Empire State Building. Could there be a more glamorous nightlight?

A colorful collection of Turkish blue-and-white pottery brings a festive air to a simple white kitchen. The border tiles are attached to the wall with double-stick tape, for easy removal if Bosquet should ever leave. Yellow flowers and towels, opposite, serve as vibrant accents in the kitchen and bathroom.

Sconces worthy of Cocteau's
Beauty and the Beast add a
touch of fantasy to the bedroom. Bosquet found them
in a Moroccan bazaar.

An illumined Empire State Building serves as a glamorous night light.

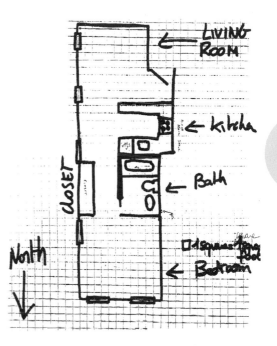

LIVING ROOM

CLOSET

kitcha

Bath

North

bedroom

500 SF

JEFFREY SHERTZ

Businessman Jeffrey Shertz has the means to live wherever he likes. Where he likes to live is in small spaces. He likes their snugness. When he first saw his present home, it was dismal and pokey, a former servant's quarters in a posh Manhattan apartment house. But Shertz perceived possibility. Living comfortably elsewhere at the time, he took on the project as a kind of hobby and, working with an architect, spent six years carefully remodeling the apartment's 500 square feet of space. In the process, he changed just

An incorrigible collector, Shertz adores living in a studio chockfull of paintings and objects.

A sculptural wood étagère establishes a formal entry, while providing display space for Shertz's large collection of *objets*. The mirrored bar is one of the apartment's many clever built-in features.

about everything from the electrical features to the walls. Believing he could arrange the layout more intelligently, he ripped out the bedroom and closet and replaced them with a small kitchen. He knocked down one of the exterior walls and put in a greenhouse. He installed a powder room where the old bathroom had been, and then built a large, luxurious master bath in the old kitchen area.

Through such alterations and additions Shertz was able to create distinct living, sitting, and dining areas, along with a foyer. He conceived these areas so they would open onto each other, giving the apartment a sense of easy flow for gracious entertaining, which is important to Shertz, as he likes to entertain at home. He's had as many as thirty people to his little home for

drinks, though he prefers to throw catered dinner parties for six. The green-house serves as the dining room, although you would never recognize its botanic origins given that its glass surfaces have been lavishly draped and hung with paintings. All the apartment's other windows are covered with blinds, too. Shertz is singularly impartial to views and natural light, which is an advantage here, as all the windows look out onto a drab interior court.

An irrepressible collector, Shertz hasn't let a lack of space limit his enthusi-asm for beautiful things. Following his heart rather than conventional design wisdom, he's covered the walls with a diverse array of paintings and photo-graphs and just about every surface with maquettes and art glass. More objects are displayed on the intricate, handcrafted étagère that separates the front door from the living area. However, in reworking the layout to cre-ate generously sized public spaces for showing off his various collections,

As the apartment looks out onto a dank interior court-yard, draperies cover all the windows, even those in the conservatory that serves as the dining room. A partial wall defines the living and dining areas, while allowing people to flow easily through the studio during parties.

164

Shertz didn't leave much square footage for such personal needs as sleeping and clothes storage, so in his marbled master bathroom, he built elaborate walnut closets, scrupulously designed to utilize every square inch of space, along with a single bed. It's an unconventional bedroom, but one that works for him.

Shertz so enjoyed the process of fashioning his highly individual home that he's embarked on the remodeling of yet another small apartment. It should be ready in a few years. Then he'll decide if he really wants to live there. So far he's quite content where he is. "It's the most peaceful haven after a day's work. One can turn on music and be in one's own world," says Shertz with a smile of serene satisfaction.

Shertz combined the bedroom, dressing room, and bathroom into one compact chamber—as efficient in its use of space as a yacht's cabin.

Dining Room Study Kitchen

Bath

Bath

Living Room

Bedroom

Bar

The partial wall, below, defines the small sitting area, while affording more display space for Shertz's collection of paintings.

A handsome Art Deco chiffonnier takes on the presence of a mantelpiece, while handily holding Shertz's extensive collection of silverware and linens.

169

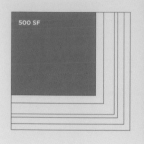

500 SF

JORDAN SCHAPS

Shortly after Jordan Schaps moved into his West Village railroad flat in the early 1980s, he noticed that many of his neighbors in the building had torn down the walls of their apartments to make minilofts. No sooner had he done the same, than he realized he'd made a terrible mistake. While the apartment *seemed* bigger, he could now see the dripping kitchen sink from his living-room sofa! He decided to put the walls back, "but nicer ones, and in smarter places," he adds. A freelance art director (he prefers the term "creative problem solver"), Schaps knows a bit about artfully arranging space. "Respect for space is almost a moral thing with me," he says. Not that he's any stuffed shirt when it comes to interiors. Above all, he wanted his renovated apartment to be "a good-natured, playful environment." And so it is.

Schaps's apartment was renovated to obtain the maximum amount of storage space. There's a wall devoted to Schaps's collection of opera recordings, as well as a series of shelves for his books on opera and dance. There are even shallow drawers beneath the upholstered banquette.

In his second renovation, Schaps was frugal with space and squeezed much more use out of it than his neighbors ever dreamed. For instance, rather than waste valuable interior real estate on a conventional bed, Schaps designed one suspended from the ceiling on a pulley system, so it could be stowed out of sight. Now he has a queen-size bed and a home-office in the very same space. The design is more than functional, it's fun. "I enjoy the muscularity of pulling the bed up and down," he says. "I get to act like Qua-

simodo!" Much in the apartment appeals to the kid in Schaps. His little office is so ergonomically snug and efficient it feels "like a cockpit." When not in his cockpit, Schaps enjoys being behind the wheel of a car. Since the days of his childhood, when his family used to make annual winter drives from Chicago to Miami, he's adored cross-country road trips. In the living room, he commissioned a wall cabinet in the shape of the United States with pull holes marking the cities in which he's lived. The dining-room table, another of his designs, has a sunken display area for souvenir shells and sand from his memory-filled Florida vacations.

When Schaps grew up, classical music and opera became his passion. They have filled not just his life but also his apartment, which brims with cassettes,

Schaps reasoned that he didn't need a desk when he slumbered, or a bed when he worked, so he combined his home-office and bedroom into a two-tiered space. By day, he has a workspace as efficiently organized as a cockpit. When he wants to sleep, he lowers his bed on pulleys attached to the ceiling.

CDs, reel tapes, and videotapes of favorite performances. He built lots of
shelving during the renovation, but he knew it wouldn't be sufficient for his
growing collection. Remembering how, as a boy, he had always wanted to
live in a home with a secret panel, he inserted one in his closet door to store
more tapes and cassettes. With the same boyish ingenuity, he turned a
heavy-duty cardboard tube used for pouring cement into a swiveling entertainment center so he could watch television from his dining table or his
sofa with ease.

Schaps upholstered the cushions on his built-in couch in a "granny floral,"
only to realize later that the tropical print, along with the room's white-
painted floor and pastel green accents, recalled the Miami of his childhood.

A secret panel within a closet door, left, reveals even more storage space for his opera recordings. What looks to be a decorative column swivels around to reveal Schaps's home entertainment center. The column is actually a cardboard tube used for pouring concrete.

"I would never wear these colors," he confides, "but they're pleasant to live in." He continued with this tropical theme when he installed wood venetian blinds and 300-watt bulbs in the window wells, so at night, when the blinds are down, it looks as if he's in a Miami bungalow with a lanai beyond.

The posters, photographs, and artwork on the walls, however, speak to Schaps's grown-up love affair with opera and dance, which is just how he likes it. When putting the apartment together, he says: "I wasn't so much interested in decorating as in personal expression." Once he expressed himself in renovating and decorating the apartment, Schaps was content to quit. He has hardly changed anything since—he hasn't had to. What brings him happiness is all around.

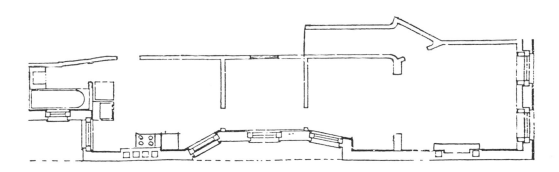

500 SF

LIVIA KAMBEROS

Livia Kamberos used to live in a New York City apartment that was so tiny there wasn't space for a dining table. "It was like a monk's cell," she says. "I like that simplicity. I can get overwhelmed by things. But my old apartment was so little, it wasn't functional." So when she came into a small legacy, she started perusing the real-estate pages. She wanted an apartment with character, high ceilings, lots of light, and room for a table and chairs. She found it on the sixth floor of an old tenement building in Manhattan's East Village. The apartment was grimy and ancient and "too masculine." The rooms were cubbyholes. But there was lots of light and views, and it was comparatively spacious. The next day she brought a friend, the architect Illya Azaroff, to check it out. "He said 'modulate,'" says Kamberos. "We did."

Although small in size and sparsely furnished, Kamberos's apartment possesses a luxurious sense of light and space.

Kamberos didn't have much money to spend on a renovation. She wanted to do the work in stages, beginning with the bedroom and living area, and then the kitchen, and then the bathroom. Azaroff treated her, nevertheless, like a potential Medici. So that she would understand the principles of architecture and its vocabulary, he gave her an extensive architectural reading list. He was shocked when she read it all. "I was such a beginner," says Kamberos with a worldly sigh. She found a kindred spirit in acclaimed architect, designer, and author Christopher Alexander, whom she quotes when discussing her ascetic inclinations: "In *The Timeless Way of Building*, he says a good home should have 'everything you need, and nothing you don't.'"

What followed was a true collaboration. "Whoever felt most strongly about something prevailed," says Kamberos. Her requests were basic. She wanted the apartment to feel open and feminine, to have ample bookshelves, and a window seat. Equally basic were the architect's proposals: rip out the old tin ceiling; tear down the wall between the living area and bedroom to open

A collapsible wall allows for the modulation of the living area according to need. A delicate use of color brings a feminine feel to the apartment, without becoming overly decorative.

the space; replace the partition with a folding wall to modulate that space; remove the pokey closet built into the bedroom and the broom closet near the kitchen; and install a single large storage space near the entry for clothes and sundry. Finally, Azaroff proposed that they construct a wall of bookshelves and place a window seat within this shelving so Kamberos could enjoy the views of the adjacent window without craning her neck.

Straightforward and efficient, these were the solutions of a Modernist, but Azaroff couched them with just enough traditional detailing to suit Kamberos's taste. For instance, he inserted panels of iridescent silk between large glass panes within the folding wall to give it texture and color. Since Kamberos liked the idea of playing up the apartment's age, he had the window frames stripped and then waxed and sealed the old wood. Kamberos went one step further and insisted the finisher leave the cracks in the panels "as is" to give the place "more character."

When the collapsible wall is closed, Kamberos has a cozy bedroom. A voracious reader, she wanted an apartment where she could enjoy her books and Manhattan's skyline views. Her vast collection serves as part of the decor.

Kamberos takes an ordered view of life. She won't be rushed when making decisions. She pondered what colors and fabrics she wanted in her apartment for a long while. She invested even more time in selecting her modest tea table and chairs. She still hasn't found just the right armchair for the reading nook, but then she's in no hurry. She's not planning on moving anytime soon.

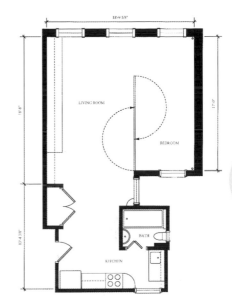

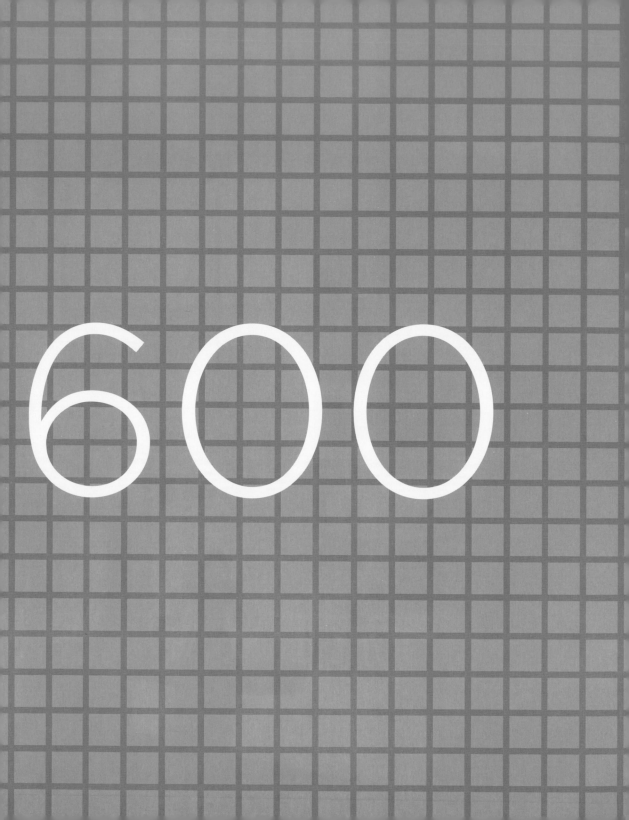
600

600 SF

SONIA HARRIS

When Sonia Harris, a graphic designer, first saw her San Francisco apartment, she knew it was for her. She admits most people might not have been as enchanted. "I can imagine them thinking, 'Oh, it's horrible!' Because it was so generic, just an open space, a blank slate," she says. There were some quirky details: lots of "odd," built-in shelving—"Great for displays!"—and a "cool bachelor's den" bedroom with carpeting on the ceiling and walls. A minus for many might have been the apartment's street-level location, but for Harris it gave the apartment a closer connection to the Haight district neighborhood she loves.

Opposite, Modern furniture classics, plucked from thrift shops, mix with campy accessories to give Harris's first-floor one bedroom a playful personality all its own.

The odd layout also suited Harris's living and working needs. A wall of shelves partially divided the main room, so a corner could serve as a distinct office. A sunny niche near the entry offered an ideal set-off space for meeting with clients. Once she moved in, "trawling for furniture" proved a slow process since Harris didn't drive. But whenever she walked anywhere she would pop into the vintage and secondhand stores along the way. Slowly, organically, the apartment took shape. "I get nuts when people organize things according to how 'things should be,'" says Harris. "This place is organized according to what works."

Harris's furniture mostly blends into the background; it's her outrageous collection of pop culture artifacts and toys that holds center stage. The London native picked up this mania from her dad, an architect, who collected packaging from the United States and pressed-metal toys (with

Superhero art, cartoon figures, a comic strip library, and a balance ball all animate this apartment. Harris used the odd configuration of walls and shelves to divide the open space into zones for work and play.

A flamboyant orange couch plays well against Harris's toy collection. It gives a bit of cheek to the informal conference area.

which he vexingly wouldn't let her play because they were "pointy"). Harris is unabashed in her enthusiasm for these objects, which line the shelves and in some places cover the walls. While most visitors are wowed by the overall effect, Harris frets they don't notice the many charmingly mischievous elements: the baby's-head knobs on the kitchen cabinets, the all-female cast of action figures adorning her conference room. "It's all in the details for me," she says.

These wild, silly objects shout "Party!" and friends and neighbors often hear the call. "There's almost always someone staying with me, and people are

Harris's well-equipped office
attests that serious work
goes on here despite the
fun and games.

A gray-and-white decor endows the bedroom with a sense of calm, while a baseball bat serves as a nod to security. The bed itself is nestled in a cave-like cove.

constantly dropping by," says Harris. "I like that. Even though I'm working here all day, I never feel superisolated." It helps, of course, that she is gregarious. She gives lots of parties—"sometimes I think I should just give up work and open a bloody salon!"—and she sometimes loans out the space to friends for their festivities. The most memorable was a bachelorette pajama party, during which some thirty young women all joined in for a game of Twister. Now that's a party palace.

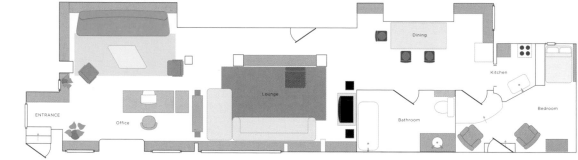

Haight Street

ENTRANCE

Office

Lounge

Dining

Kitchen

Bathroom

Bedroom

Key

windows

shelf or ledge

door

Harris used mirrors in the kitchen to give a feeling of openness to the otherwise tight space.

Some people line their walls with framed etchings, while Harris prefers packaged action figures.

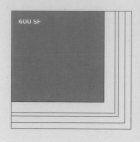

600 SF

WILL VAN RODEN AND ANTHONY LEE

When Will Van Roden and Anthony Lee found their New York City apartment, no bells and whistles went off. They liked the West Village neighborhood, the duplex layout, and the back garden, but what they liked best was the low rent. Otherwise the place was rather generic. Then again, they like generic; in here, they have turned it into a decorative leitmotif. Take the series of basic white medicine cabinets you're greeted by upon entering their minuscule kitchen. The arrangement is so determined in its banality it might be taken for installation art. In fact, it's storage for glassware, spices, and, appropriately enough, aspirin. Or consider the stacked rows of aluminum cans in the bedroom, which look almost Warholian in their silvery plainness. They neatly serve as storage for such everyday flotsam as pens and pencils, electric sockets, and pull hooks.

A wall of basic, white medicine cabinets provide witty storage for kitchen essentials.

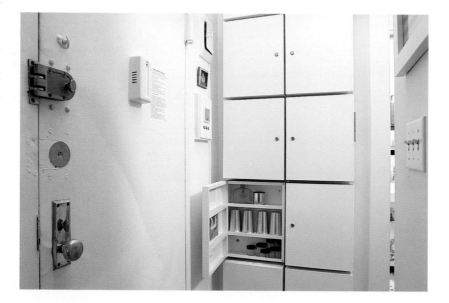

Van Roden and Lee collect everything from packaging to mid-century Modern furnishings. Sometimes their collections are casually displayed, while other times they are placed in contrived settings. The surprise and delight of this interior comes from the balance between the two.

Storage doesn't have to spoil a room's ambiance. Neatly labeled plastic bins on the top bookshelf blend in with books and boxes, thanks to their utilitarian design and ordered arrangement.

A geometric-patterned quilt brings a homey touch to a brilliant red, but rather minimalist Eames sofa. The two gave a new spin to an old family ottoman by attaching industrial wheels to it. The myriad recordings, housed in the bookshelves, blend into the room's decor because they read like a single entity.

To save space, Lee and Van Roden positioned a shelf over the stairwell to accommodate their stereo system. Their television fits neatly beneath it. Bamboo steamers serve as decoration along the stairwell's ledge, as do an assortment of old wrenches.

Making a game of aesthetics is a way of life for these two: Van Roden is a
graphic designer; Lee is an architect. Nevertheless, there is an aesthetic
code to which they hold fast: that of stripped-down, functionalist Modernism. It's why, long before it became a style mania, the pair were scouring
city streets, flea markets, thrift shops, and upstate New York vintage furniture stores in search of midcentury modernist works by such masters as the
Eameses, Eero Saarinen, Alexander Girard, and Eva Zeisel. They have scored
abundant finds. "We have enough chairs in storage to furnish a country
house," jokes Van Roden. In the beginning, though, they made do with
literally what was around: they put casters on an simple hand-me-down
ottoman to give it a fresh spin; they recycled a thick pile of the *New York
Times* into a side table by neatly cutting the papers, skewering them with
metal poles, and then screwing on wheels and a laboratory top.

You might say they've curated rather than furnished their apartment, since
everything seems to be part of some kind of collection or series. In the
bedroom, for instance, Lee's collection of old typewriters runs whimsically
across one of the walls, and their cases line the shelves below, serving as
stylish storage for magazines and papers. The small scale of the rooms only
intensifies these conceptual symmetries. The studied nature of the rooms
and the everyday subject matter of the art collection work a certain dead-
pan magic so that a trio of Rolodexes on a shelf take on the aura of art.
The happy paradox of this generic equation is that it reveals the singular
humor and edgy intelligence of the uncommon pair who dwell here.

Old-fashioned typewriters
are an unconventional adorn-
ment for a wall, especially in
a bedroom, but that's what
makes them such a witty decorative detail. Their black
cases, situated in the bookshelf below, serve as storage
for magazines and papers.

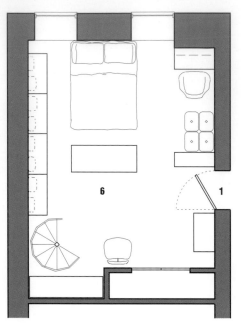

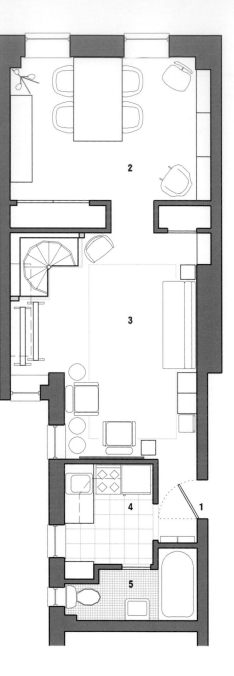

1   ENTRY
2   STUDY / DINING
3   LIVING
4   KITCHEN
5   BATH
6   BEDROOM

Even the most banal objects,
like these empty paint cans,
can become design state-
ments when arranged in a
series. The appeal of their
repetitive form is doubled by
the storage they provide.

Anthony Lee (left) and
Will Van Roden

WING CHAN

Wing Chan, a graphic designer, had lived quite contentedly in a small studio in Manhattan's West Village until he decided to go freelance and work from home. He tried to make a real home–office, building a loft bed, and putting his desk and files underneath. But with his bed so close, siestas became a distracting routine. To make a success of his business, Chan would need a larger space so he could put some distance between himself and his slumbers.

He spent about six months searching for the perfect one-bedroom, and when he had about given up hope, a 600-square-foot one-bedroom became available in his own building. What could be more perfect? He loved the building, his neighbors, and the doormen. But he knew he couldn't convert the apartment into a professional workspace on his own; he needed

When a small space is both home and office, finding a way to clearly define the two is central to a pleasing interior design.

an architect. He'd long been impressed by an imaginatively conceived stationery boutique in his neighborhood. The various papers were all attractively stored in a wall of shelves visible from the street. He was intrigued by how the architect had combined the roles of storage and display. As soon as he had placed a deposit on the apartment, he rang up its architect, Roger Hirsch.

When Chan and Hirsch met, they clicked right away. Chan explained that he needed a separate office space, distinct dining and living areas, tons of storage, and—what he liked—minimalist interiors. Hirsch went off to the drawing board and came back with a prop and a proposal. The prop was an old-fashioned extending wood ruler. Inspired by its neat ability to fold and expand, Hirsch had designed a long rectangular wooden box with a retractable wall. The box would separate Chan's living and sleeping areas from each other, and house within it his office. It would be big enough for workstations for Chan and an assistant, with lots of space left over for files and archives, and a computer, printer, and scanner.

One of the cleverest aspects of the structure is the way the panel opens to frame the living area's window, letting in light and views. The other side of the panel serves as a bulletin board.

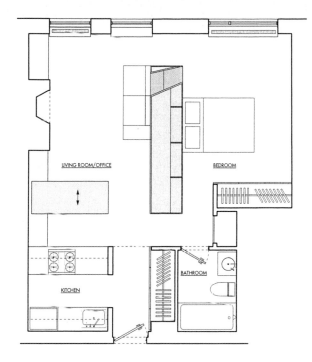

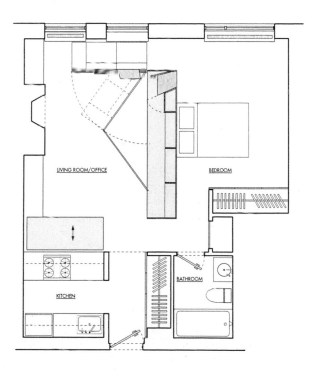

As Chan had requested, Hirsch scoured every inch of the apartment for extra storage space. He found a spare few inches next to the HVAC unit to neatly shelve Chan's photo albums and a niche next to the chimney flue into which rolled drawings and plans could be tucked. He designed Chan's bed with a set of commodious drawers. Playing with the notion of retractability, Hirsch installed a dining table supported by a wheeled leg and a track built into the side wall. When Chan is working, he can slide the dining table against the wall; when he's entertaining, he can pull it out so his guests can sit around it. Hirsch inserted a data grommet in the adjacent wall cabinet to make it possible to neatly set up a workstation at the table for another assistant if his business grew—it has and he did.

The dining table is on wheels so it can sit either against the kitchen wall or be rolled out when guests come to dinner. There's a data grommet in the side cabinet, so the table can serve as an extra work station.

A small ledge above the fire-place provides just enough space to prop up art work.

Chan speaks gushingly about his apartment and its many space-saving wonders. He grew up in Hong Kong in a tiny chaotic apartment with eight siblings, six of whom all slept in one bed! To have an apartment of his own that expresses his love of order and detail is a long-dreamed-of delight. His greatest pleasure, he confesses, is when he slides the wall to his office shut at the end of the day and finds himself once again in his serene and simple living room.

A deep opening in the structure makes it feel less like a solid block.

Small spaces can never have too much storage: the built-in bed features drawers below it; beneath a window ledge a narrow compartment holds photo albums.

A well-organized closet helps
keep Chan's wardrobe orderly.

A fold-out shelf serves
as a night table.

600 SF

LOTTA JANSDOTTER

When, six years ago, Lotta Jansdotter, a Swedish-born surface designer, was deciding whether to rent a one bedroom in an old Victorian building in San Francisco's Haight district, the old-fashioned bathtub with its lion-claw feet was the bit of charm that clinched the deal. In truth, her little apartment fairly oozes charm *and* character with its big fireplace and mirrored mantle, built-in cupboards with stained-glass detailing, coffered ceiling, and elaborate wainscoting and moldings. Its personality is all Jansdotter's, though.

Attractive kitchen and table-ware don't have to be hidden. Here, they make the kitchen feel welcoming and easy.

When inexpensive furniture—much of it here is from Ikea and flea markets—is mixed with pretty accessories (like Jansdotter's pillows) the overall effect can be charmingly personal.

Her contributions by way of furnishings are modest, many of them Ikea purchases, and a few choice flea market finds like her antique brass bed. But these, mixed together with the pillows of her design and personal arrangements of favorite objects, endow the small set of rooms with a feminine spirit and spontaneous warmth. Adding color came later to her decorating and was something Jansdotter embarked upon with trepidation, first painting the bathroom blue, but was then something she tackled boldly, painting her bedroom lavender and her kitchen a brilliant Chinese lacquer red. "It's constantly Christmas in the kitchen," she says.

Light, space, and a flowering plant give this unassuming bathroom charm.

An old butler's pantry now serves as a study. The orderly arrangement of the books, boxes, and office equipment makes the little room feel nestlike instead of cramped.

Until recently, Jansdotter lived and worked in the apartment, so she needed a lot of storage space. A wooden flat cabinet for keeping her textile designs doubled as her coffee table. The old butler's pantry served as her office. Now that her boyfriend Nick Anderson has moved in, the space has evolved again. She's set up a storefront studio for her business, and Anderson, an architect, has taken over the pantry as his study. He came with lots of books, so the couple invested in more bookshelves. They now line the walls of the study, a model of spatial efficiency. More shelves fill a wall of the bedroom. Jansdotter says a closet of "quality junk" had to be dispensed with to make way for Anderson's clothes, a worthwhile trade by her lights. Living in small spaces is a continual study in give-and-take.

The couple love to cook and have friends over. Dinners for eight are a regular event. On these occasions, a folding table and chairs, kept in the closet, are set up in the living room. Jansdotter has a global repertoire of favorite recipes, but friends are partial to her meals of split pea soup and pancakes, the traditional Thursday night fare in Swedish homes. She's also famous for her cinnamon buns.

Adorable as her little apartment is, Jansdotter admits that there are some drawbacks to living in such prettily detailed antique spaces. "Things are constantly falling apart," she says. "The mantelpiece is charry from the new heater!" she laughs. "You get used to it, though. It no longer matters that nothing's quite perfect!"—a wise philosophy for life, no matter how big your home is.

A tall bookshelf, densely packed with books and storage boxes, emphasizes the ceiling's height when a low table and pillows are placed nearby.

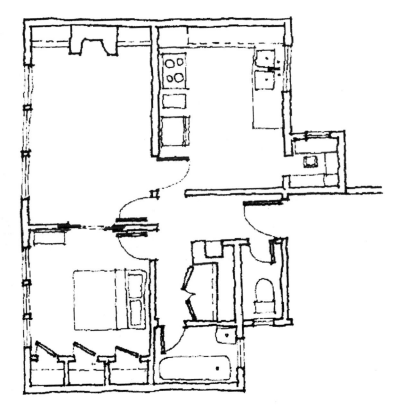

An antique bed frame heightens the Victorian detail of the bedroom, as do the mauve walls.

Jansdotter's pretty fabric carryalls serve as unexpected storage compartments within her closet.

750

750 SF

RUBY LERNER

When Ruby Lerner, the director of an arts organization in Manhattan, came into a small legacy, she went apartment hunting and happened upon "the deal of the century." Despite the attractive price, other buyers had passed on this one-bedroom, apparently unable to see beyond its dismal brown walls, meager daylight, and prison-style bathroom. But at 750 square feet, it was palatial compared with the shoebox in which Lerner was then living, and she knew a pair of architects capable of miraculous transformations.

Not long before, Frederick Biehle and Erika Hinrichs of New York City–based Via Architecture had remodeled Lerner's former office. It was the first time she'd ever worked with architects, and the experience was a revelation because it was such a close collaboration. She enjoyed the creative dialogue concerning everything from aesthetics to work habits that is so central to

Jewel tones, soft and hard forms, and a low wood bench together bring a lively spatial complexity and sense of fun to what might have otherwise been a forgotten corner of the living room.

One of the best strategies for maintaining an orderly home, especially a small one, is to have lots of places to stash stuff. This foyer is lined with cabinets for just that purpose. Their non-uniform sizes and sponge-painted texture make them a lively decorative element.

A cast-off radiator became a sentimental object to Lerner during the renovation. When she had it marbleized to match the floor, it became an *objet*.

the design process. While they were Minimalists, the architects respected Lerner's traditional streak. Their gift for interpreting their clients' needs and tastes through their own vocabulary was apparent in the results. "I loved turning the lights on every morning," she recalls. Best of all, they accomplished their design magic on a shoestring budget.

When the three met to discuss her apartment renovation, Lerner had some straightforward requirements: replace the depressing galley with a proper kitchen and breakfast nook, overhaul the bathroom and install a whirlpool tub, and give the place some architectural complexity. Then she got personal. "I am a slob," she remembers confessing, "and I'm not going to stop being one. But I don't want other people to know." Designing an apartment that would be mess-proof became core to the architectural *parti*. As with Lerner's old office, the budget was modest.

By adding and shifting some partition walls, the architects were able to fulfill all of Lerner's requests. First, in the entry, they built a wall of bins in which Lerner could, if she liked, throw her stuff. (She liked and she does.) As the bedroom was overly spacious, they moved the dividing wall farther into the bedroom by three feet so that there would be room for a distinct

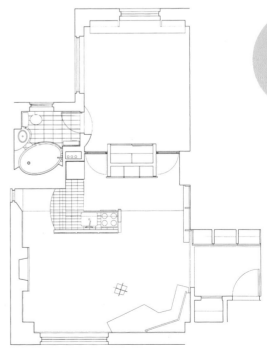

An unassuming mirror above
the mantelpiece opens up
this pretty, feminine living
room. The folk art and crafts
scattered about give it a
quirky edge, as does the
capricious spacing and shape
of the bookshelves.

kitchen. They then installed more storage bins on both sides of it. To separate the kitchen from the living area, they constructed an L-shaped partition wall around it. In a corner of the living room, they built a low seating platform to create a multilayered sense of space. Though filled with furniture and devoid of a real view or much natural light, the room still feels open, largely because of the spatial variety. While in her previous apartment Lerner seldom had anyone over, here she finds the space so friendly and easy she's boldly entertained some thirty people for dinner.

Lerner wanted architectural complexity, so among the architects' many small interventions is a congé above the bathroom door. It has no structural use; it's there solely for Lerner's visual delight. Inside the bathroom, there's enough "surprise and hazard" to make that fabled architect of complexity

Small spaces always benefit from some transparency. Partial walls separate the kitchen from the living room and the living room from the bedroom, which enhances the apartment's sense of flow. A see-through niche in the kitchen wall affords glimpses of the activity within.

Sir John Soane smile. The sensuous, oval-shaped Jacuzzi engages the
concave above-counter basin and the irregular rectangles of the medicine
cabinet in frolicsome geometric play, making the bathroom the liveliest
room in the apartment.

It's no surprise then that Lerner misses the creative interaction with Biehle
and Hinrichs. "It was like an art commission," she says, straining to explain
the intensity of her involvement. Her consolation is her lovely, fanciful home.
"I couldn't be happier," she says, truly beaming. "I feel as if I'm living in the
middle of a sculpture."

There is method to the erratic
placement of handles on the
kitchen cabinets and the
eccentric collection of forms
in the bathroom: they inject
some jazzy personality into
otherwise cramped rooms.

Mirrored panels behind the illumined glass bookshelves open up this small, viewless bedroom and bring an extra sparkle to the objects on display.

800

800 SF

STEVEN SHORTRIDGE

Steven Shortridge had been living in Venice, California, for a number of years when an upheaval in his domestic arrangements resulted in his looking for a place to live on his own. Remembering a long-empty bungalow in the neighborhood, he decided to investigate. It had, he discovered, suffered its own domestic separation. It began its life as part of a house—the front parlor and dining room, to be exact—in nearby Pasadena before being cut off in the late 1930s and carted away to Venice to serve as a makeshift beach house. Later, a kitchen and a laundry room were tacked on.

Charmed by its curious history, Shortridge, a partner in the Culver City architecture firm Callas Shortridge, thought he could make this architectural fragment whole. While preserving its past, he wanted to update its form.

In warm climes, living areas can extend outside. A walled-in patio doubles this bungalow's living space. The greens and oranges of the garden's plants and the building's facade are carried through the interior.

Although it was a relatively modest project, Shortridge says the architectural issues were the same as those he deals with when designing substantially larger houses. At the crux of both is the need to create an appealing sense of space and flow.

Shortridge began by reorienting the building so the entry would be through the living room, not the front parlor. He then reworked the layout so that every room would have "a duality of use." In what had been the front parlor, he conjoined the work and sleep areas; in the hallway, he installed a row of closets, drawers, and cabinets; and in the former back room, he melded the living and dining areas. So that the house would feel more airy, Shortridge

The organic forms of the mid-century Modern furnishings soften the bungalow's angular geometries.

The original kitchen was left
intact, its quaint fixtures
enhancing the cottage's
charm. The window frames
are painted a Zinnia hue,
which runs as a leitmotif
through the interior and
exterior rooms of the house.

The bungalow's old bath was
salvaged, but the rest of the
bathroom was entirely
redone. A drain inserted into
the floor encourages bathers
to splash away without
regret.

Deep drawers and roll-out
shelves were installed in the
discreet alcove leading to the
bathroom, creating a semi-
private dressing area.

raised the ceiling from eight to ten feet and finished it in tongue-and-groove Douglas fir to match the existing window frames and flooring. He brought in more light by installing a clerestory window in the bedroom and a skylight in the bath. Respectful of the original detailing, he extended the bungalow's vintage baseboards throughout, retained its breakfront dining room, and salvaged one of its sliding pocketdoors for closing off the bedroom–office area. Through these gentle interventions, Shortridge transformed the bungalow into a place of light and air and playful geometries.

In true Californian fashion, Shortridge extended the house's living space into the outdoors by turning the former backyard into an open-air great room. He installed a raised plinth on which he set a concrete terrace, and then walled the patio with bamboo, ficus, fruit trees, and palms and an imposing steel-plate fireplace. What's a great room without a great hearth, after all? As the house's exterior was now part of his living space, he gave it a makeover as well. He replastered the bungalow in a cayenne shade, the

color inspired by an old bougainvillea vine in the yard. He removed the slanting tile roof and installed a sloping aluminum and fiberglass canopy that lets rainwater run down the drainpipe and spill melodically into the terrace drain during thundershowers.

Shortridge likes to entertain—he's had parties for as many as seventy people—and the easy flow between indoors and outdoors encourages guests to mill all over. As his kitchen remains small, and his time precious, he leaves the cooking to caterers. Once forlorn and abandoned, this amputated bungalow is now people-filled, sunny, and utterly whole.

A wood partition encompassing bookshelves, drawers, and a sleek desk divides the bungalow's former front parlor into an office and bedroom. By not extending all the way up to the ceiling, it enhances the multi-windowed room's sense of airy openness, while affording a degree of privacy.

Shortridge's workspace is
compact, but feels roomy
because it is open to the
rest of the room.

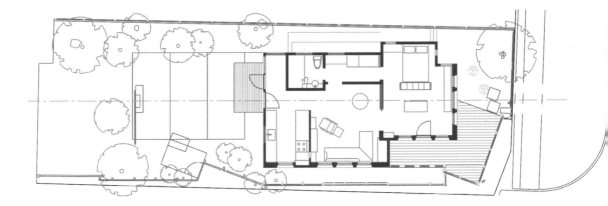

800 SF

DEBORAH OROPALLO AND MICHAEL GOLDIN

During the early years of her career as a painter, Deborah Oropallo lived in her studio with bare-bone domestic comforts. "A hot plate and a toaster oven" is how she sums it up. She had no real furniture. Her surroundings were unimportant; her focus was her art. She did, however, covet a building, an old factory with fifteen-foot ceilings and glass-brick windows. When it came up for lease, she convinced the owner to sell and so became a home-owner—of sorts. Oropallo demolished the interior and parceled out to friends sections of the space to be used as offices and studios, keeping just 800 square feet for herself for living and working.

Soon after, she met her husband, Michael Goldin, an architect and furniture designer, and things began to get domestic. Well, sort of. All over the ceil-

From the moment she first saw it, Deborah Oropallo knew that this old factory building was her dream house. Years later, she and her husband, Michael Goldin, an architect, turned the building into a friendly, if unconventional, family home.

ing, Goldin punched out skylights, flooding the building with light. A former chef, he installed a professional kitchen and a nine-foot dining-room table. "Food became the center of everything," says Oropallo. "Michael made it nurturing." When their first baby, Leo, came along, Oropallo gave up her small office so he would have his own bedroom. When their daughter, Gina, was born, Goldin tore out some of the shelving he had built and constructed a mezzanine to serve as bedroom and playroom for both children.

Goldin is also a trained chef; his professional kitchen is the heart of the house. Antique restaurant furnishings bring a battered warmth to the industrial space. A French plate stand, left, provides a bit of Gallic flair, while keeping dishes at the ready.

A children's play zone is distinguished from the main living area by brightly colored furnishings, a balance ball, and gymnastic rings hanging from the ceiling. Almost all the home's furniture is on wheels so it can be reconfigured according to changing needs.

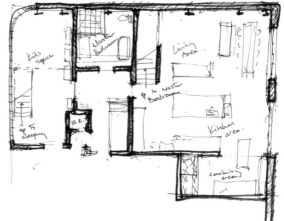

Before the couple had children, the bookshelves extended up to the extra-high ceilings. When kids came into the picture, Goldin sliced away a section of the space to construct a mezzanine, which now accommodates a bedroom for them and for him and his wife. Densely lined with possessions, the wall of shelving takes on an architectural presence, and so avoids being an eyesore.

The bathroom is no-nonsense in its accoutrements, but the shower curtain and rug add a sense of fun.

As the couple put a high value on creative freedom and flexibility, having a space like this that can be endlessly reconfigured is a joy. Goldin brings this ad hoc approach to his design work, especially his furniture business. His company Swerve is known for its series of simple and colorful tables, equipped with industrial wheels. They have been designed to get pushed around, both at home and at work. Oropallo shares her husband's utilitarian approach to furniture. A pair of metal lockers in her studio recently did a tour of duty in the kitchen when extra storage was needed. Another pair now serves as toy storage in her children's room. From the couches in the living room to the kitchen worktable, everything in the house moves around—Goldin has put it all on wheels. While some of the furniture is industrial, and the arrangement improvisatory, the atmosphere is surprisingly homey. Colorful rugs, pillows, objects, and an assortment of artworks by Oropallo and friends bring warmth, personality, and fun to the space.

In this unconventional dwelling, the central gathering place is not the hearth—there isn't any—or the dining table, but an upright piano (on wheels, of course) with Goldin's electric guitar hanging next to it. Oropallo grew up in a home full of musicians, and she wants music to fill her children's lives as well. By having instruments out where the family congregates, instead of a television, the hope is they will start making music together. By the looks of their home, they already are.

A Tibetan meditation rug brings an air of fantasy to the children's room. Heavy velvet draperies transform their bunkbeds into a secret hideaway.

800 SF

LAURA HANDLER

When Laura Handler bought her first apartment, she turned the 400-square-foot unit into a little jewel. No sooner had she effected this transformation than she realized she did not want a precious gem. What she wanted and needed was space—to breathe, to laugh, to live! (This is a woman who vacations in Alaska.) In New York City, of course, space comes at a premium. Handler couldn't afford lots more than she already had. Being a designer,

Neutral tones and clean lines pull together the many eccentric objects in this droll, light-filled living room.

Rather than have a wall of
books distract from the
serene order of the room,
Handler hid them behind a
curtain, mimicking the cur-
tained window on the other
side of the room.

When renovating the apartment, Handler had a niche cut out of a closet for her entertainment system, so it wouldn't become added furniture in the room.

Handler calls the dining area her "front porch" because it looks out on the street—though from the 18th floor! The fanciful polka dot upholstery of the banquette and the subtle dado of gray-and-white paint distinguish the corner from the rest of the room. Adding to its whimsy is her pairing of a halibut trophy from an Alaskan fishing trip with old family photographs.

By inserting a bookshelf in the side of a wall, Handler cleverly keeps her book collection concealed from view.

The decorative motif of black and white runs through the apartment. Here, black and white kitchen cabinets are conjoined and given a touch of luxe by a splashboard of black-veined white marble.

however, she knew that well-laid-out open spaces with views could make not-so-big apartments feel grand. So she went apartment hunting, again.

She discovered a diamond in the rough: a one-bedroom in Manhattan's Chelsea. "It was hideous," says Handler, "everything was a disgusting brown and smelled like cat!" Most prospective buyers couldn't see—or smell—beyond that. But what Handler sniffed out was an apartment twice the size of her current home, with windows in every well-proportioned room. She especially liked that the living area had a corner with two exposures, and a view that stretched from the verdant terrace of her neighbors all the way to the flashing lights of Times Square.

"I thought I'd make this my porch," she says. She painted the top half of the corner walls a pale gray and the bottom half a white to distinguish it from the rest of the apartment, and built banquettes on both sides. She upholstered them in polka dots. "I can't help it," says Handler. "It's unintentional, but everything I choose always has a sense of humor about it."

Handler started out working with an architect to help renovate the kitchen, combine two closets into one walk-in, and rework the bathroom. But she ended up finishing the design on her own. "The architect didn't listen," she explains. "All the ideas were too fancy. I wanted bare bones, but good

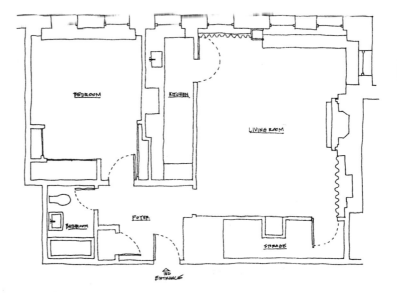

Danish Modern sconces,
grandma's bedspread, and
hand-me-down Colonial armchairs keep happy company
in Handler's bedroom. One
trick to her idiosyncratic decoration is, again, the mixing
of black-and-white motifs
with neutral elements.

bones." Fancy became fanciful. Handler's wit is everywhere to be seen: in the playfully arranged standard black-and-white mosaic tiles in the bathroom and in the wry vignettes adorning the walls and surfaces.

Handler mixed modern and traditional furnishings, not so much by design as improvisation. Her beloved dining chairs are vintage George Nelson, her coffee table classic Eero Saarinen. But the wing chairs in her bedroom are from her mother's home—"the only pieces that didn't have American eagles on them, and they're comfortable!" she says—and her crochet bedcover is her grandmother's. How does everything work so well together without a plan? Perhaps because she's a designer, Handler edits her purchases subconsciously. In any case, the apartment continues to evolve. "I change things all the time, according to what I buy," she observes. "Sometimes I don't know what I'm going to do with something, and put it away till I figure it out. My only rule when it comes to decorating is that I don't buy anything that shows dirt!"

800 SF

THOMAS DANG VU AND ALLAN KAM

Thomas Dang Vu and Allan Kam left Manhattan for the outer boroughs of New York City in search of a yard. When the two were children—Dang Vu in Saigon, and Kam in Honolulu—they each had one. Their families considered them urban necessities, sanctuaries from the rush of city life, a place to work the earth and see things grow. Happily, they found just what they were looking for in Brooklyn: a big, neglected yard attached to a first-floor one-bedroom in a row house.

At 800 square feet, the new apartment was spacious enough to be transformed into a little world unto itself. However, when they began decorating, Kam says, "it seemed more about Thomas's vision than mine." A nostalgic

Inside a Brooklyn rowhouse, Dang Vu and Kam have recreated a little corner of colonial Saigon.

Dang Vu sought to conjure up the colonial Vietnam of the 1950s, doing up the interior with yellow walls, green shutters, and white trim. "Then I thought, 'Oh, Asian tropical, that's me, too,'" says Kam. "Because I'm Chinese."

Together they painted the apartment and installed the parquet wood floors. But it was Dang Vu, a professional stylist and a former decorative painter, who distressed the living-room wall to evoke the picturesquely crumbling facades of Vietnam's old colonial houses. He also supplied much of the furniture. While the two antique Chinese cabinets, the many Chinese chairs, and most of the artworks were bought from the shops of friends, most of the other furnishings, including the church pew in the living room, he scavenged from off the sidewalk in front of a funeral home in his old Chinatown

An assortment of tropical plants, bamboo blinds, green shutters and a wall full of photographs of modern ancestors makes for a convincingly Vietnamese-style room.

neighborhood. Songbirds in delicate cages, lots of tropical plants, and a scattering of Asian musical instruments—all of which he plays—complete the atmosphere he's created.

As both young men are tea connoisseurs, they assembled their own traditional Chinese tearoom. Together they built the sideboard, where they keep their tea cups and pots and an assortment of rare tea leaves, crafting it from antique wood so it would resemble the dry goods storage cabinets found in Vietnamese courtyards. The shelving they made out of old Chinese wine cartons and an antique jewelry box.

Songbirds heighten the Oriental ambiance. Dang Vu used a decorative painting technique on one of the walls so it would resemble the picturesquely crumbling stucco of Vietnamese houses. An antique Chinese chest harmonizes surprisingly well with a Scandinavian Modern chair.

The hanging shelves in the tearoom were made out of an old Chinese wine carton and jewelry box. The sideboard with its metal-screened doors is a common fixture in Vietnamese households. The pair assembled it out of antique wood and wire mesh.

A section of a Chinese screen sets the stage for an Asian vignette, replete with songbird cage and porcelain Buddha.

In the backyard, Kam, who trained as a landscape designer, helped Dang Vu re-create the Saigon garden of his childhood memories. It features a philosophers' stone and koi pond, which represent the symbolic mountains and water that are essential to every classical Chinese garden.

With its tea chests, bonsai, and songbirds, this home may seem as carefully propped as a movie set, yet there's nothing stilted about it. When a friend or two drops by, the couple brews some tea. If a group comes for dinner, Kam prepares some Hawaiian dishes. During the summers, they go out back and barbecue. Daily life for Dang Vu and Kam is a fusion of East and West. Just don't expect any hotdogs at their summer shindigs. How about some lemongrass chicken on skewers instead?

An Asian lute placed casually on a chair completes the bedroom's decor.

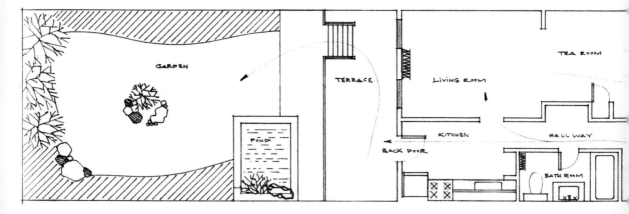

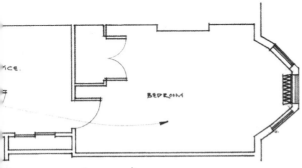

The pair transformed an over-
grown backyard into a Chinese
garden, reminiscent of the
one Dang Vu left in Saigon.
This one, though, has many
of the same Hawaiian plants
from Kam's family's backyard.
During the warmer months,
the garden serves as an outdoor living room.

RAUL CABRA, LUIS CATALA, AND MICHAEL SLEDGE

During the dot.com frenzy of a few years back, the rent on the San Francisco office of Raul Cabra's graphic design firm more than doubled. So Cabra decided to invest in a building where he could have both his office and home. In the Mission, he soon found an old four-story Victorian-style building. The only hitch to his real-estate maneuvering was that he had recently settled into a big house in nearby Oakland with his Labrador/Doberman mix dog, Walter, and a roommate, his friend Luis Catala. He would be scaling down from a 4,000-square-foot house to an apartment of some 800 square feet!

Mid-century Modern furniture pairs happily with the wedding cake architecture of this San Francisco Victorian.

Seldom has a moving experience been so suspenseful. "I kept measuring and remeasuring my dining table," says Cabra. "I was so worried that it and my other furnishings wouldn't fit." He packed all his spare furniture (there was a lot, Cabra is a flea market enthusiast) into storage, taking only his living, dining, and bedroom furniture. Everything just fit. Cabra credits this mini-miracle to the neat proportions of his furnishings, most of them mid-century Modern pieces. He had started trolling the many vintage furniture stores in San Francisco for these works long before they were popular. "They represent the narrative of my life, the stories of where I got them and how," he notes. The furniture also seems ideally suited to his taste—and habits. "I can't sit still," Cabra confesses. "It's my nature. I'm always moving things around until they feel right. That's probably why I became a graphic designer. And this furniture is so light you can rearrange it without the help

The room's personality comes not so much from its furniture as from its accessories, including flea market vases, Eva Zeisel tableware, and little statues of the cult Venezuelan saint José Gregorio Hernandez.

The apartment came
equipped with a Murphy bed.
As it's not in use, its closet
has been turned into a tiny
study; the bed's frame now
serves as a room divider.

A sparkling tangle of Christmas lights gives a festive air to a physician's stainless-steel cabinet.

In addition to mid-century
Modern furniture, Cabra
collects contemporary Bay
Area design, works like Jeff
Covey's stool.

A multitude of windows creates a feeling of openness in this compact kitchen. Inexpensive shelving from Ikea keep utensils and tableware orderly and close at hand.

of a friend." He was happy to discover that its clean, spare lines engaged the wedding-cake architectural detailing of his new Victorian home in a convivial dialogue.

Nearly ten years ago, Cabra's admiration for mid-century Modernism inspired him to design a chest of drawers for his bedroom. When he went searching for a fabricator, he discovered that the Bay Area was chock-full of small contemporary furniture companies. Soon he was amassing pieces of this furniture, too. His bed, the stools in the kitchen, and most of the lighting fixtures are all by local talents. Like the masters of mid-century Modernism,

these designers were making works that were spare, flexible in function, and mobile. Such qualities served Cabra in good stead when he fell in love and his new boyfriend, Michael Sledge, moved in to the already tight quarters.

Cabra's ingenious arranging has made it all work. Needful of a desk, he inserted a narrow table into the alcove reserved for the living room's unused Murphy bed, creating a discrete home-office. When there wasn't room for a Christmas tree in the cramped living room, he put bunched strands of mini-lights into a glass-paneled cabinet for some festive illumination, and liked them so well, they became a permanent fixture. And he brought just

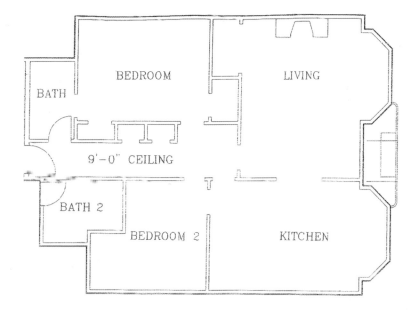

Catala's unassuming bedroom has a certain design flair thanks to its savvy arrangement of decorative and everyday objects. The wood cabinet's varied shelving makes it a witty display case.

enough of his various collections—Eva Zeisel tableware, flea market glass vases, and Magrittesque figures of the Venezuelan cult saint José Gregorio Hernandez—to lend the surroundings some quirky distinction without overwhelming his housemates with a determined style. Thanks to these light touches, three men and a dog have succeeded in living in cramped harmony together.

Blond wood furnishings and picture frames pull the decor of Cabra and Sledge's bedroom together. As Cabra is forever composing vignettes of everyday objects, he designed a chest of drawers with a glass compartment on top, so he could display his still lifes without using up counter space. All the room's artworks come from flea markets.

Flowers enhance the prettiness of this pale, simple bathroom, which has the luxury of natural light.

800 SF

BERT LONG AND
JOAN BATSON

When he was an architecture student at Houston's Rice University, Brett Zamore thought it sad that there were so many derelict shotgun houses in Houston neighborhoods that needed good inexpensive housing. The shotgun is, after all, a classic Southern architecture type; its lineage can be traced from the bayou back through the colonial sugar plantations of Hispaniola to West Africa. A linear, single-gabled wood bungalow with one of the earliest known examples of a front porch, the shotgun was well suited to southern climes: it was set on blocks so air would circulate below the floor

A festive array of artworks—
many important African
pieces—endow this modest
Shotgun with life and style.

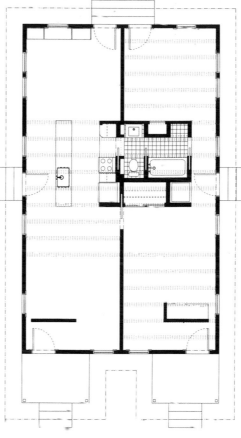

House 00 Floor Plan

for cooling; and its aligned front and back doors, when opened, promoted ventilation. But because shotguns served as housing for slaves on Hispaniola's sugar plantations and then for freed slaves in the South, most African-American Houstonians shunned them.

Zamore decided to restore an abandoned shotgun in Houston's Fifth Ward district for his senior thesis as a way to further explore the vernacular. He hoped that by rethinking the house, he might get locals to give it a fresh look. In his reconstruction, he ripped out most of the house's interior walls and its low-dropped ceiling to open the interior. Zamore wanted its new owner to define the space. His renovation coincided with the Fifth Ward's own redefinition. Once a thriving African-American neighborhood and a

The well-stocked kitchen is
the heart of this house, which
is appropriate as Long first
distinguished himself as a
chef, before embarking on
a career as an artist.

When towels and bathroom
sundry are neatly stored,
there's no need to conceal
them.

To heighten the aura of this shotgun's history, the closet door has been stripped down to its original wood. The exterior plank-wood wall has also been left unpainted.

fabled center for the blues and jazz, it had become known as "the Bloody Fifth," distinguished only by its staggering poverty and murder rate. Now revival efforts were under way.

Bert Long grew up in the neighborhood, but life took him far afield, first in his work as an executive chef, and then as an acclaimed artist. But two tragedies, the destruction of his house in a hate crime, and then, two years later, the death of his wife, left him feeling adrift. He decided to come home. He wasn't a stranger. He'd been involved in community revitalization projects and his sister and mother still lived in the neighborhood. So Long bought Zamore's reconstructed shotgun; he loved it for its architectural invention and its mottled past. It was, for him, a way to reconnect with his roots as a Fifth Ward native and an African American, and to cultivate new roots as a local artist and role model.

When Long returned, it was with a new companion, Joan Batson, whose life has been as surprising as his. A Scottish-born art conservator and painter, she lived for many years on a kibbutz before coming to the States. Themes

A partially walled, L-shaped desk provides work and storage space, while containing it from the entry's view.

of community, preservation, and cultivation have run through both their lives, and now, in their new home, they are being woven together. Though modestly furnished, the house is exuberantly trimmed with plants and art—works by Long, Batson, their friends, and Long's lovingly assembled, extraordinary collection of African pieces. The heart of the house is its well-stocked kitchen, appropriate enough for a former chef. However, the soul of the place may be the backyard garden. Long talks as enthusiastically about his 200-pound Carolina Cross watermelons and Tiger tomatoes as he does about his rare beaded Cameroonian stool. "Food and art are what it's all about," says Long, who's working on a performance piece that combines the two. "This house reflects our life. I always tell people, 'your home is your castle. Here's your opportunity. You don't have to be rich to express yourself.'" In the Fifth Ward, thanks to Zamore, and Long and Batson, one shotgun house in Houston has become a model home.

800 SF

KEN KENNEDY AND JUDITH CURR

When Ken Kennedy and Judith Curr, husband and wife, moved to New York City from Sydney, Australia, they found an apartment in one of its most picturesque neighborhoods, Beekman Hill. Its winning feature was its panoramic views of midtown Manhattan, stretching from the East River to the Empire State Building. Otherwise the apartment offered little besides its convenient location—little, indeed. It was a cramped two-bedroom with low ceilings, "useless closets," and an unworkable kitchen. The couple realized at once that to open the space, bring in more light, add more storage, and redo the kitchen, a gutting was in order.

A wood cube containing a walk-in closet makes for a dramatically long entry hall, creating anticipation for what's to come.

10 MITCHELL PLACE

They didn't shy from this major undertaking. Kennedy, an architect, took on the redesign himself. By reworking the layout into fluid zones of living and sleeping, he conceived an interior that is flexible, easy, and finely attuned to the couple's way of living. He placed the living area in the sunny front of the apartment with its exceptional views, and put the sleeping area in the quieter back. A maple-clad box that houses the walk-in closet separates the two.

The living and dining areas flow into each other, enhancing the sense of openness. But as the couple entertain a lot, they needed some delineation between the two activities. So Kennedy designed freestanding I-beam-shaped bookshelves, open at the top and bottom to suggest a boundary. Bookshelves were a necessity as Curr is a publishing executive, and placing them in the middle of the room freed up the walls for emphatic displays of their small but deftly curated collection of Australian art.

Kennedy extended the kitchen cabinets into the living room to provide more storage. As they are almost flush to the wall, they blend in to the room's geometries. He carved out niches in the walls and inserted uplights to give added dimension to the space.

The hall opens onto the living area and its views of the United Nations Building and East River. Bookshelves divide the living and dining zones.

A sculpture of corrugated metal in the shape of Australia serves as a reminder of the couple's native home.

The kitchen was completely
scrapped and reorganized, so
it could be an efficient work
area with enough counter
space to prepare real meals.

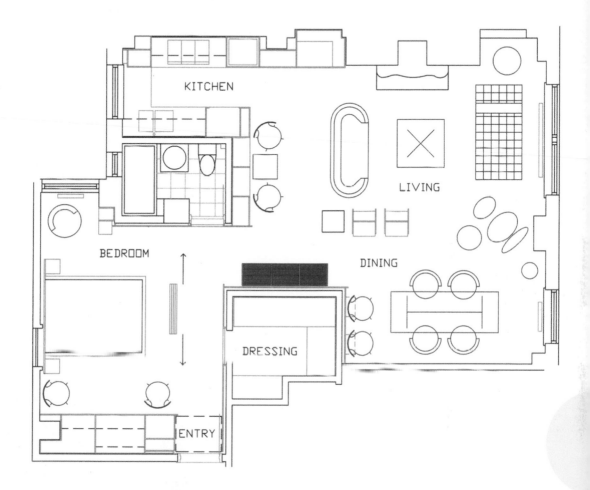

KITCHEN

LIVING

BEDROOM

DINING

DRESSING

ENTRY

In each room, the ceiling's elaborate beamwork frames a single patch of vivid color harmonizing with its featured artwork.

The existing galley kitchen was too narrow and crowded with appliances, and there was hardly any counter space. Kennedy ripped out everything, installing sleek new appliances and a stainless-steel counter. To make up for the storage lost in this alteration, he subtly extended the kitchen out into the living area—the refrigerator straddles the two—and lined its adjacent walls with ample cupboards.

The bedroom was just puny, so Kennedy ripped out the wall that bordered the entry hall, replacing it with sliding walnut panels. Now the sleeping zone can open into the hall when the pair is home alone, or, when guests come over, it can be closed off by sliding the panels shut. Kennedy also inserted a wall of cupboards for added storage, even making room for a small stowaway office.

Richly colored paintings and furnishings bring warmth and delight to the spare decor. One of the bedroom walls is lined with cabinets, which hold not only clothes, but also a small pull-out office.

The apartment was designed to be as open and light as possible. But in every home, privacy is also a requirement. When seclusion is desired, wood panels slide across the open hallway, walling off the bedroom.

The couple wanted rich color in the apartment but Kennedy worried that strongly toned walls would pull down the low ceiling, which already felt heavy because of its elaborate beamwork. Here, the problem became the solution. In each area Kennedy painted one of the framed ceiling panels a vivid hue. Color became a way to further define the apartment's various zones and give vibrance to the low ceiling. Each of the tones he selected picked up on or contrasted with a color in an artwork below. The couple's selection of lively upholstered furnishings has introduced more splashes of brilliant color into the apartment. Yet nowhere does the apartment seem dominated by a particular hue.

Out of what was once a cramped, old-fashioned space, Kennedy created an airy, gladsome interior as sleek and sophisticated as his adopted city, yet in the palette of his native land.

900

900 SF

MARK RABINER AND AVI PEMPER

Mark Rabiner and Avi Pemper had already lived in several apartments together when they bought a dingy, dinky two-bedroom in Gramercy Park. Why? For its absolutely spectacular terrace and splendid city views, they say. The purchase marked a turning point for them in regard to what they wanted in a home. "We'd always decorated our apartments in a very safe way. We choose identifiable furniture and recognizable art," says Rabiner. "This time we were no longer worried about getting things right, we wanted

A startling combination of colors and textures energize this minimalist interior.

To increase the amount of
natural light in the apartment
and to make the most of its
views, the exterior wall separating it from the terrace was
replaced with floor-to-ceiling
sliding windows. Inside and
outside now blend together,
an unusual effect in a city
apartment.

Different hued neon lights, installed above and below the kitchen cabinets, control the mood within this otherwise stark galley kitchen, conceived more for drama than for serious cooking.

Luminous white tiles, brilliant strips of incandescent and fluorescent lights, and vivid red accessories make for a cinematic bathroom, worthy of Kubrick.

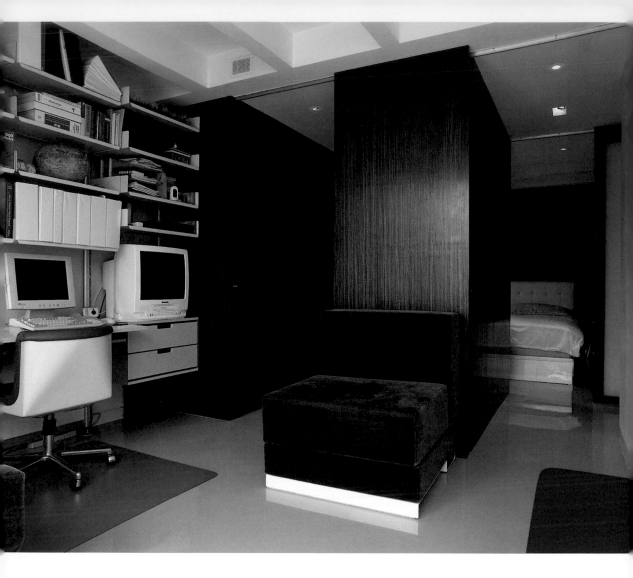

to express ourselves." They had, says Rabiner, "evolved in their tastes." While aesthetics are important to both men, they are especially so to Rabiner, a physician who treats the homeless. Since his days are spent making "house calls" to the denizens of shelters and flophouses, he needs beauty when he comes home in the evening. "It plays a big role in my happiness," he says.

Rabiner selected David Khouri of the New York City design firm Comma to design the apartment because he had always liked his orange acrylic Puzzle Screen. Khouri's work pushes the envelope, which was where these

The study can be closed off to serve as a guest room. The austere but cushy velvet lounge chair unfolds into a bed.

The different natural patterns of the woven grass wallcovering, combined with the wood chest of drawers, imbue the bedroom with a subtle richness.

two had a mind to go. Khouri says the couple gave him free rein in conceiving the apartment, telling him only that they "wanted a place where they'd feel so great, they wouldn't want to go away on weekends." As the apartment was postwar, he reinterpreted the indoor/outdoor California architecture of that era for sophisticated urban living. The apartment's exterior wall bordering the terrace was knocked down and replaced with floor-to-ceiling windows opening the apartment to the Zen-inspired garden on the terrace and the Manhattan skyline. Like the California homes of the postwar period, the apartment's new layout followed an open plan.

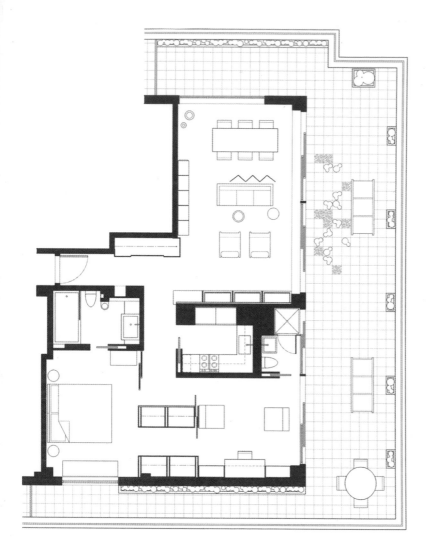

The grasslike wooly runner in the entry plays counterpoint with the apartment's many sleek, shiny surfaces.

From the beginning the pair welcomed Khouri's adventurous suggestions, but as the design process went on, they became downright intrepid. "They were willing to try a poured epoxy floor, which I'd never done before," says Khouri. "When choosing a color, I showed them several muted blues, as well as the turquoise they then selected. I don't know if I would have been that daring." For Pemper, a financier, the choice was obvious: "The only thing this apartment was missing was water." As Pemper's favorite color is orange, the living room features furnishings in various orange tones. Combined with the turquoise floor, it's a courageous combination. To make up for the apartment's lack of architectural detailing, Khouri selected unusual materials such as the luminous white structural glass tile in the bathrooms and the East Indian rosewood on the living room wall unit and bedroom closets, endowing the rooms with greater visual interest and complexity.

Both Rabiner and Pemper concede that some of the apartment's experimental elements might not work for less disciplined residents. Everyone must step out of their shoes upon entering the apartment and don slippers so as not to scuff the delicate epoxy floor. The gleaming white kitchen and bathrooms may afford high drama, but they are also high maintenance. The minimalist aesthetic means that everything needs to be in its place—all the time. "If I leave my clothes on a chair, it ruins the design effect," admits Pemper.

If the apartment is a little precious, its owners insist they aren't. They are, says Rabiner, "jeans, white T-shirts, and flip flop–kind of guys." When they entertain, which is often, it can be for forty friends—"from every walk of life." Dinner is usually great take-out served on the terrace. Neither of the two likes cooking, but Rabiner laughs that he's "very talented at laying out the food, so it looks beautiful." They may be neat, but they're easy.

A shower in the guest bathroom opens out directly onto the terrace, so sunbathers can step in for a quick cooling spritz.

The terrace, about the same size as the apartment, is where the couple prefers to entertain.

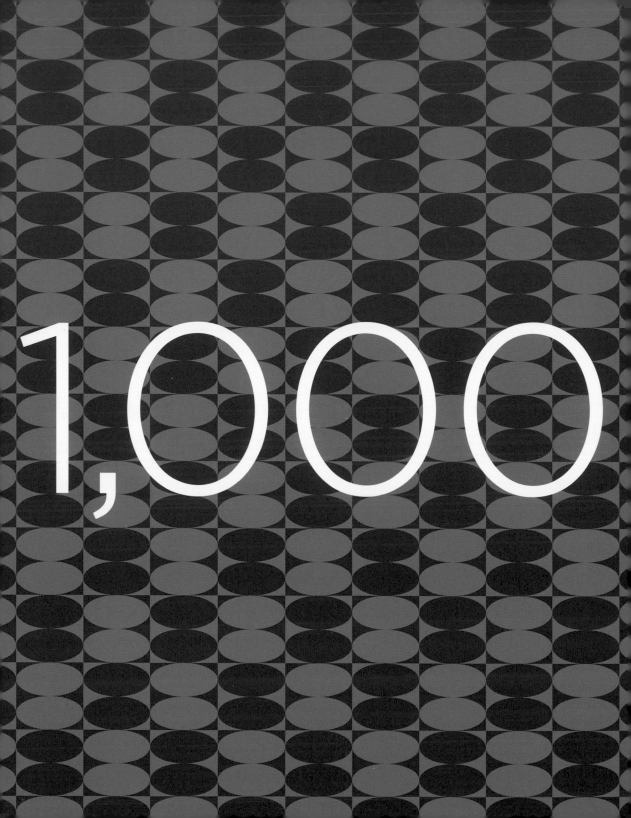

1,000

1000 SF

MICHAEL WEBB

There isn't a design aficionado who wouldn't covet Michael Webb's Los Angeles apartment. The building was designed in 1937 by Richard Neutra, the celebrated Austrian émigré who helped define California living through his open-to-nature architecture, and the apartment was the first California home of Charles and Ray Eames, whose work has come to define American Modernism. What's now Webb's office was once the Eameses' workshop, where they set up their "Kazam" press and began experimenting with bent plywood. The rest, of course, is design history.

The organic forms of the furnishings engage the "cool geometries" of the architecture in lively dialogue.

A strong design vibe still seems to animate the place and its occupant. When some twenty-five years ago Webb first moved to Los Angeles and leased his apartment, it was to work for the American Film Institute. But before long he'd returned to his earlier career as an architecture and design writer. Starting anew, Webb lived at first with a minimum of furnishings, content with the fine proportions of the space, the abundant light, the verdant views, and the luxury of being able to have the windows open most of the year—an especial delight for a native Londoner.

Over the years, though, the apartment's energies seem to have taken full possession of him, and Webb embarked on what has been a slow, often meandering journey of home design, during which he's amassed an intriguing collection of art and craft as well as furniture. While he's taken his time, he hasn't been without a decorative plan. He wanted, he says, "to foster a dialogue between Neutra's cool geometry and the organic rigor of the Eameses." He also wanted each of his three rooms—office, living room, and

The air of spaciousness here is enhanced by Neutra's appropriation of a ribbon window, which runs across the apartment, opening the rooms to the outdoors.

One of the Eameses' early bent plywood splints hangs above their famous folding screen, also made from bent plywood. Webb's smart positioning of the folding screen—behind it is a freestanding head-high storage closet that faces the doorway—gives definition to the entry, dining, and living spaces of the apartment.

bedroom—to be distinct. "If only to avert cabin fever," chuckles Webb, who sometimes when writing doesn't leave his apartment for days on end. Serendipity has also played a role in the design, as his selections have often arisen out of his journalistic research and travels, like the aboriginal painting he bought when visiting Australia, or his collection of lights by Ingo Maurer, about whom he's written extensively.

So immersed is Webb in design culture that he points out that the color of the file cabinets in his celadon-hued office is "the Cherokee red that Frank Lloyd Wright popularized," then adds that "the room's shelves were made by Frank Gehry's favorite carpenter." Gehry's deliciously loopy bent-plywood chair is a featured ornament in this serenely rectilinear room, as is Webb's impressive collection of turned-wood vases. In keeping with his plan, "sensuously rounded" furnishings abound everywhere. In the white-stucco-walled living room, there are chairs and screens by the Eameses, an armchair by Alvar Aalto, a tubular metal sofa by Gilbert Rhode, "sexy" side chairs by Philippe Starck, as well as a truncated oval dining table.

But it's in his bedroom that Webb's passion for design is at its most bold. During a trip to the Netherlands, Webb was captivated by the early-twentieth century Dutch art and architecture movement de Stijl, especially movement leader Theo van Doesburg's café in Rotterdam. When he returned home, he painted each wall of his bedroom a different primary color. What might seem overwhelming to some, Webb finds happily reassuring. "Waking," he says, "I feel I'm in a golden cornfield, with a clear blue sky above and a comforting red glow behind me." Now, is this not a man possessed by the Modernist spirit?

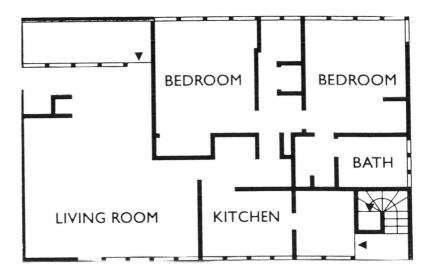

A brightly colored chair and poster enliven this small alcove.

Webb had shelving and a desk built-in around the perimeter of his designated work space. The efficient storage system provides an organizing structure for his reference books and ample display space for his collection of turned-wood bowls, while not overwhelming the room.

The bold palette of the de Stijl inspired Webb's daring bedroom decor.

A few brightly colored bowls and plates accent the sparkling whiteness of the charming vintage kitchen.

KEIRA ALEXANDRA

One day while riding home to Brooklyn on the subway, Keira Alexandra looked up just as the train emerged into daylight and spied for the first time a tall factory building wrapped with giant ribbons of windows. She'd never noticed it before. "What an amazing place to live," Alexandra remembers thinking. It looked like an industrial building, but she decided to check it out anyway. Now Alexandra calls a loft there home.

When explaining the raison d'être, if you will, behind her extraordinary apartment, Alexandra starts out by talking about herself as a child, about

The incongruity of the objects is what makes Alexandra's "groupings" so amusing and, sometimes, mysterious.

The clean, understated lines of Alexandra's furniture add a twist of irony to her campy displays.

how she wanted to be a window dresser. "Ever since I was six or so, I've made groupings," she says. "It started with little Fisher-Price people." It hasn't stopped. She became a graphic designer, a career that extended her hankering for making arrangements to the printed page. In the privacy of her home, she continued to make vignettes. You might say that her whole loft has become a considered display. When she moved in, she installed long rows of shelves in the kitchen and in the sleeping area for exhibition purposes and tore down a partition wall to enlarge the living room so visitors would get upon entering the full gestalt of her myriad assemblages.

This brings us to the other key aspect of Alexandra's penchant. In order to make groupings, it's necessary to have objects to group—in Alexandra's case, many, many objects. She chooses the most humble, commonplace, ephemeral, and kitschy. They speak to her, especially those that are plastic, or colorful, or interestingly shaped, or even better yet, all three. She attributes her most unnatural aesthetic to being a reaction against the purist, monochrome Modernism of her parents' house. (She admits, though, that "everything that is tasteful here, I stole from my mother.")

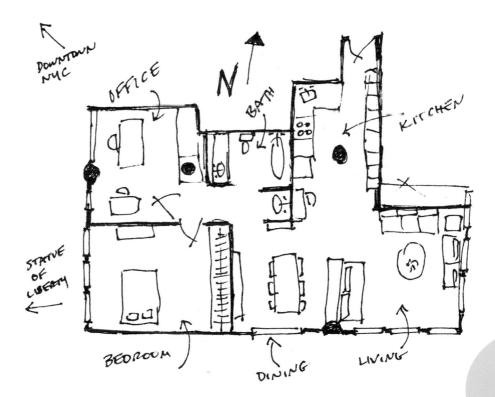

367

The power of Alexandra's displays is due in part to their sheer number. Repetition also plays a role. Her rotary phones serve as a kooky, decorative leitmotif throughout the apartment.

Alexandra can't help making groupings out of her colorful clothes and putting them, too, on display.

Alexandra calls her arrangements no more than "nicknacking," but there is art among the artifice. Through her inspired curating, the unexpected beauty, humor, and emotion of these objects often become manifest. Sometimes, though, her assemblages simply highlight the wonderful silliness of daily artifacts; other times, they work more like wallpaper, endowing a dull space with color, texture, and interest.

What pleases Alexandra most is the pleasure friends reap in exploring her vignettes. She fantasizes about someday opening a museum of miscellany so the world can enjoy her discoveries. In the meantime, her loft gives blithe, new meaning to the phrase "museum-like home."

ANTONIO DA MOTTA AND
ROBERT KETTERMAN

"The apartment chose us," says Antonio Da Motta of his Los Angeles home. The Brazilian-born interior designer had been living in Manhattan for many years when he was offered a job in California. When he and his boyfriend, Robert Ketterman, tentatively went apartment hunting, this was the first apartment they saw: a one-bedroom in an early 1920s Spanish Colonial with windows on three sides, in their favorite neighborhood, and on the prettiest street. Call it kismet. So long, Big Apple.

An eclectic collection of
furnishings and art gives this
apartment a sophisticated,
cosmopolitan air.

Da Motta designed the elegant glass screen and whimsical wood chest in the dining area. Their refined proportions complement his assemblage of vintage furnishings from the 1930s and '40s.

In New York City, Da Motta was adept at decorative condensation. He lived in a small but high-ceilinged loft with chopped-up rooms and huge, blank plains of wall. The apartment was, in other words, absolutely devoid of architectural distinction. To make up for this lack, Da Motta created an intense Latin baroque interior, with deep-hued walls, elaborate drapery, eccentric paintings in ornate frames, antique religious art, and his own urbanely exotic furnishings. In short, he broke the rules of just about every design authority as to how to make the most of an odd, pokey layout. His decoration may not have made the space feel larger, but the effect was grand.

When he migrated west, he brought most of his furniture and artworks with him. However, the look of his home changed dramatically. His new apartment had architectural character. It had fine proportions, a lovely layout, nice moldings, and, being L.A., lots of windows. It also had plenty of closets. Da Motta even liked the oyster-white walls. But he does love color, vivid color. Ever since he was a child, Da Motta has had a red room, so he painted the bedroom's ceiling red. Arranging the furniture and choosing some simple, diaphanous window treatments were the only other decorative chores Da Motta had. The effect is still dramatic, and eclectic, but more casual—like Los Angeles itself.

Da Motta grew up in a house full of art, which from an early age he was responsible for curating. It's hard for him to imagine living in a home without it. While his artworks obviously serve as decorative elements within his home, he respects them as serious creations. Unsurprisingly then, he has strong feelings about how they should be displayed. He dislikes the current trend of hanging similar images in a series of matching frames, believing that this treatment causes the individual works to lose their import. Instead he likes to frame and arrange his pieces so that they are as interesting singularly as they are in a grouping. He takes a similar approach to his furniture

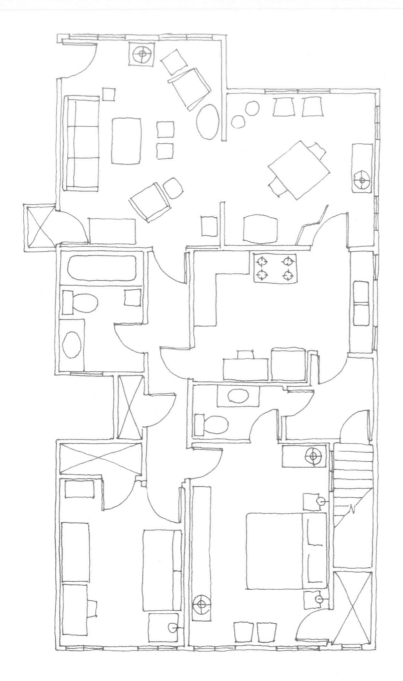

The interior's design is an
orchestrated composition
of biomorphic forms, cool
geometries, lush patterns,
and rich colors.

arrangements, mixing big and small, tall and short objects and furnishings. It gives a certain sense of liveliness to a room. It's in a similarly impromptu spirit that he sometimes simply props artworks up against the wall along the floor. "The result may not be as finished," he says, "but it forces you to look more at each piece."

When it comes to entertaining, Da Motta and Ketterman are enthusiastic and convivial hosts. They often have dinners for six to ten people, but as their dining table seats only four, guests are given big napkins and eat in the living room buffet-style. Informality is the rule here. "I cook without stress," says Da Motta in a deep, languorous voice. "The food is often Bahian. People love the mix of influences and ingredients, Nigerian and Portuguese, cloves and cinnamon, yucca and coconut milk." The sophistication and appeal of Da Motta's cooking seems natural. You have only to look around the apartment to see that he has a way with blending unusual elements into something rich, intriguing, and utterly delectable.

Wood columns in the dining room give greater distinction to the interior's architectural detailing. The wall behind the sofa is covered with paintings in a variety of sizes to encourage visitors to study each work.

A crimson ceiling and vividly patterned textiles enliven the bedroom without over- whelming it.

Robert Ketterman (left) and Antonio Da Motta

1000 SF

KAREN MEYER

When Karen Meyer bought her Greenwich Village apartment, she knew from the start that a major renovation was in her future. She loved its big terrace, but she wasn't so keen on its confining rooms and worn-out kitchen and bath. What she desired was an apartment that would have "a one-space feel." She was excited about creating her own environment, but a little nervous, too. "I'd always lived in rentals, and had never done anything with my apartments before," she says. Meyer interviewed a couple of architects but

It only requires a few well-chosen pieces of furniture to make a room inviting.

The apartment was laid out in
a way that provides easy flow
between the living room, dining room, and kitchen.

felt that their styles were too distinct from her own. She wanted an interior designed according to her style of life and personality. Happily, Meyer, the head of human resources for a major bank, had a good friend who was an architect, Ted Porter of the New York City firm Ryall Porter. Porter was more than willing to design an interior that suited her taste and life. "It was very much a partnership," says Meyer.

If there is a theme to this renovation, it is flexibility. Porter did more than give Meyer an interior with "a one-space feel," he also gave her the alternative of intimate rooms. Meyer likes to give small dinner parties; she also likes to have friends over to play the card game euchre. Porter reconceived the

When guests stay the night,
the living room is closed off
via glass partitions and the
dining area's wall of books
slides across the room to
seal off the kitchen hall and
reveal a Murphy bed.

layout so Meyer would have a distinct dining and card-playing area within the larger flow of the living space. And she can convert her dining room into an enclosed second bedroom by sliding forth some wood-framed glass panels to wall off the living room and by shifting a bookcase to close off the hallway to reveal a Murphy bed.

Meyer likes contemporary design, but she didn't want anything too trendy in her own home. She and Porter selected pieces that were "sleek and comfortable" with classic lines. The kitchen verges on the austere, but its warm cherry cabinetry and illumined cabinets endow it with a welcoming glow.

Luminous glass panels add interest to a sparely furnished bedroom. When parted, they reveal an enviably generous closet.

A band of color and illumined opaque glass cabinets high-light the rich tones of these custom-made cherrywood kitchen cabinets.

Luminous green glass tiles in the master bath bring a shimmery softness to its contemporary design. In the bedroom, the same glass panels framed with cherrywood that partition the dining area here close off the enviably generous main closet. Clean-lined, open, flexible, and welcoming, Meyer got an apartment that's just her style.

Pale celadon-hued glass tiles and a matching glass sink add to the appeal of this simple, but luxuriously equipped bathroom.

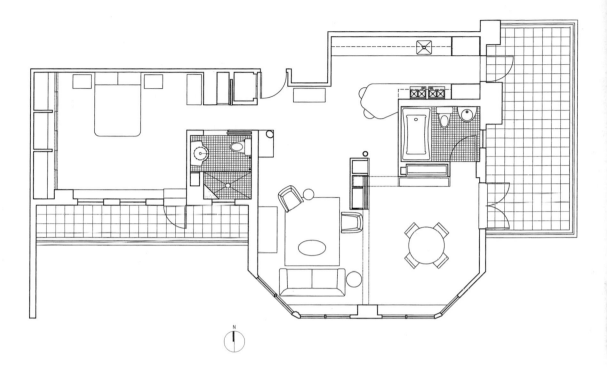

the end

Directory of Featured Design Professionals

pp. 18–20
Yolande Daniels and Sunil Bald
Studio Sumo
101 West End Avenue, #7S
New York, NY 10023
studiosumo@rcn.com

pp. 52–61
Christopher Coleman
Christopher Coleman Interior Design
70 Washington Street, suite 1005
Brooklyn, NY 11201
718-222-8984
ccoleman1005@hotmail.com

pp. 72–79
William Stewart
William Stewart Designs, Inc.
349 Peachtree Hills Avenue, NE
Atlanta, GA 30305
404-816-2501

pp. 82–93
Stuart Basseches and Judy Hudson
Biproduct
236 West 26th Street, suite 604-A
New York, NY 10001
212-255-3033
www.biproduct.com

pp. 140–147
Francisco Pardo/Ximena Orozoco
at 103
103 Prince Street, Studio 4M
New York, NY 10012
646-613-7047
pardo@at103.com

pp. 176–181
Illya Azaroff
The Design Collective
212-219-3248
iazaroff@aol.com

pp. 194–207
Anthony Lee
32 Leroy Street, #1
New York, NY 10014
917-757-5255
email.lee@alum.mit.edu

pp. 208–214
Roger Hirsch
Roger Hirsch Architect
91 Crosby Street
New York, NY 10012
212-219-2609
www.rogerhirsch.com

pp. 232–243
Frederick Biehle and Erika Hinrichs
Via Architecture Studio
198 Broadway, suite 800
New York, NY 10038
212-227-5832
ViaFB@aol.com

pp. 246–257
Steven Shortridge
Callas Shortridge Architects, Inc.
3621 Hayden Avenue
Culver City, CA 90232
310-280-0404
www.callas-shortridge.com

pp. 258–267
Michael Goldin
Swerve
2332 Fifth Street
Berkeley, CA 94710
510-644-1898
www.swerveco.com

pp. 308–317
Brett Zamore
Carlos Jimenez Studio
1116 Willard Street
Houston, TX 77006
brettzamore@hotmail.com

pp. 318–329
Ken Kennedy
10 Mitchell Place
New York, NY 10017
212-753-1204

pp. 332–347
David Khouri
Comma, Inc.
149 Wooster Street, suite 4-NW
New York, NY 10012
212-420-7866
www.comma-nyc.com

pp. 372–381
Antonio Da Motta
M/dM Concept
1560 South Beverly Glen Boulevard
Los Angeles, CA 90024
310-551-1816
mdmgroup@sbcglobal.net

pp. 382–393
Ted Porter
Ryall Porter Architects
135 Fifth Avenue
New York, NY 10010
212-254-1175
www.ryallporter.com

Credits